Me,

Peter Jackson 1927

Our home,

Mother, Edith

Father, J James

GEMS OF THE PAST   by Peter Jackson.

I first saw the light of Day in one of two small Cottages, near Bullfa Grove, on the outskirts of the Village of Gunthorpe; Norfolk. Borne with the privileges bestowed to those during Chime hours claimed my Mother, with pride.

With the exception of a Family by the name of Knox, there were no near Neighbours. A small lane from the cottages to the road; at that time, was made up of stones and Marle.

At this junction a large woodland. From this early stage was in the Care of the National Trust and known as Bullfa Grove.

I have very little recollection of our stay at Bullfa Grove, though the impression of the place has stayed with me all my life, and the building block to the path; I was, !though not always possible, preferred to follow.

My Brother was borne a year later in the June. And together Mother wheeled us in the Pram around the lanes when she was able.

Mother loved Bulfa. We played in the leaves in front of the log Cabin; that was in the Grove, a shelter for !whoever wished to rest a while. Mother walked us up to the Railway Crossing; Gates on the Thursford road, just to see the trains pass through.

The year Nineteen twenty-seven. Father had no employment, he gathered shellfish on the marshes and peddled them around the Villages. He was a very smart young man. Presentable and had worked at times in the Feathers Hotel in Holt.

He found work from time to time in the Hotel's at Sheringham. Thereby, connections with the golf Course; often found him in demand as a Caddie.

Sometimes he brought home a small toy for us, much to the Dismay of mother. !Who found it difficult to make what little they had, pay their way.

Mother gathered water cress from the stream in the meadow near to the house. Father set snares for rabbits, on the land by the lane.
Should one have caught a rabbit, Mother soon covered it with grasses until Father returned to retrieve it.

Water had to be fetched from a well; we shared with the Family next door. The Closet "Toilet". Quiet a walk down the garden, it contained a wooden bench seat, with a hole in the top to sit over. Below the hole, the Pail; that had to be emptied in the garden.
Squares of paper threaded on a string, hanging on a nail in the wall by a box, Containing; Candle and Matches.

All in all, it was a struggle for them in those early days. This was just after the general Strike. The local Authority had a few schemes to get men working. One was breaking stones by the side of the road. For "Road repair". It cost Father more for the protective glasses he had to purchase, than he was able to earn. Though he did say. "One man with the knack of finding the grain of the stone, would shatter them with one tap and was able to make a fair wage".

Father

Father was offered the fire wood from a very high hedge, in a field near to the house. Should he care to cut it for the local farmer.

With his slasher; and me toddling by his side, started to work on the hedge. Not aware of the danger. I was close by and was struck by the back of the Axe as he took a swing.
I am to understand that, he lifted me up in his arms, ran over the field jumping the roadside hedge, some four-foot-high; and to the house. Where he left me in mothers care while he cycled to Sharrington for the District Nurse.
I was bound with bandages for many weeks and lucky not to have lost my sight.

I remember my grandfather and Grandmother coming over from Briston, with my Sister. They brought my Sister up. Grandfather was a Guard on the Railway, I being his first grandson he was very concerned.

Those early days; I remember little of.

The Airship R101 came very low over the grove and scared me to the extent; of implanting R101, in my memory way before I was able to read.

Mother Weekly walked to Langham, to do a day's washing for her Mother. She was paid Two Shillings and Sixpence for that, the bonus was; my brother and I were treated to food, and one day less for Mother to struggle finding something to fill our stomach's with.

It was on one of these journey's, Mother had the close encounter with the Sharrington Ghost.

Father always a man to keep up with the times. We had a Crystal Radio set he and his father had made. It had to be concealed in the wall oven, it not being in use at the time, what little they had to cook could be heated by the small fire grate. During this time and having Children he was able to apply for Parish Relief from "The Parish Officers", The Chairman being one of the local Dignitaries. The Parish Chairman, being responsible to the Walsingham Rural District.

This Relief of course was means tested, before any payment was made. All that could be sold had to go first, they had a few Chickens, but told the Authorities they were his neighbours. After all, the value of the Eggs, came to more than the relief money.

You may have no more than the clothes you were wearing, and a week's food in the pantry. Then Parish Relief may be paid. Equivalent to day of about, Ten Pence.

Many of the old people who were now in need of help, had given their limbs for their country in the first world War. And those who had given their lives. Their families found it even more difficult; as they had no one to challenge the Authorities.

For Mother; sadly, comes the day. The end to our stay at Bullfa Grove. Grandfather had a house vacant at Briston and wanted Father to move and live there.

Before we leave Bullfa Grove, I must tell you, "Mothers encounter with the Sharrington Ghost".

Mother had completed her day at Langham; the weekly wash for her mother. Safely tucked the hard-earned Half Crown in her purse, put my brother and I into the pram, made her goodbyes to her Mother, and started the journey back home to Bullfa Grove.

The darkening sky, and cool breeze, offered not one of the best of day's Mother had trudged those weary miles, five or six at least of twisting partly made roads. She was on the way through Sharrington, it was starting to rain, the sky had turned from a dull grey to blue black, in the distance a sharp crack of lightening followed by the thunder, as it seemed to pass overhead. A large farmhouse and yard to the left very inviting. Mother and we two boys in the pram, took refuge in the open cart house; of the stables in the yard. The Storm was getting louder and was turning the whole Farmyard into night.

In desperation Mother pushed her charges up to the Farmhouse door. Hardly had she lifted her hand from the door Knocker; the door opened, and the lady of the house stood in the doorway. "Oh, do come in dear she remarked", without being asked. "He is playing up something terrible today, it is the storm it always makes things worse".

Mother pushed the pram into the warmth of the large kitchen, her charges having now dropped off to sleep. Slowly realising that the lady of the house, was referring to a supernatural Being, not her "Husband as she first thought. Became very interested, taking the hospitality the lady offered, was quite willing to listen while she related her story.

"We do not always hear It", she said. But during times such as this, it really gets angry, and move everything upstairs to where it wants it.

"It started some years ago, just after the two boys had started work". The oldest going out in the evening", she said. "Often there was some trouble when the older boy came home, the younger said he had pulled the clothes off the bed.

My family with nanny [me on the far right.]

Sometimes the bed was moved across the room, other times the bed was striped, having been made up during the day. In the end it has been better to leave the bed making until after four O'clock.

"May! I have a look" Mother said. After some thought the lady agreed, they went up the winding stairs to the boy's room. It was at the top of the stair, and a door to the left, a door in front of them, and to the right on the open top stair way the boy's double bed.
Looking to the door to the left Mother said. "What is in there? looking through the large cracks between the boards, seeing the light from a small window, showing up the dust laden room with very little in it. The latch handle was chained. "We have never opened it" the lady said, the door in front of them was the same. "When it is really bad"; she says, "to go to their bed before ten O'clock; is impossible. Its throw's the chains off the first door, goes over to the bed throw everything on to the floor, throw the chains off the other door. Then all is peaceful for days. Sometimes; Months".

Mother looked again into booth rooms. It was plain to see; that If only a small object moved in that dust and cobweb laden room, it would have left some trace.

The storm had cleared, Mother now on her way home with her; still sleeping charges. Tingling with things she had seen and heard, and the story she had to relate to her dad, next time they go over to Langham. My brother and I slept peacefully through it all.

In the village of Briston, where Hall Street meet the Stone Road. In the late Eighteen Hundred the Railway line through to Yarmouth needed to cross the road, Stone road; It appears was slightly diverted to make way for the Railway Crossing, and A Gate House with Crossing Gates.

At this juncture, a Loke leading to my Grand Fathers cottages, closed to the road with a large gate and lined with a tall hedge, and poplars on one side. There were Orchards on either side of the Loke.

Our new home was to be the first Cottage one of two, my Grand Father living in the larger property set aside from the Cottages.

Next door living a Mrs Ducker. I remember very little of the Lady, only we had to share a toilet with her. This was out the back and in its early days had been an earth Closet, now modified to take a toilet bucket, this still had to be removed and emptied in the garden.

Mrs Ducker was very fond of her front Flower garden and may be seen when it was favourable with a lighted candle after dark, hunting slugs and snails.

The imagination may run wild as to what a spectacle this would present to the unwary onlooker. To see the bent over figure, a hand at ground level illuminated with the light from a yellow; wavering flame.

Our first stay in Hall Street hold few Memories for me. Grand Father passing the cottage wheeling his Cycle, in his Railway Guards uniform, a large wicker food basket mounted on the carrier, he often found a sweet from within. We saw little of Grand Mother, even when going to the well for water. The well-being outside her house.

I understood she did query, why! anyone needed to have more than one pail of water in any one day, even on wash day. Though Mother always used Rain water. It was "Much softer she said".

My Sister lived with my Grand Parents, she had nice things and they were very fond of her. Grand Father called her "Will". I often wondered why?

There is a dispute in the Family, and Father decided the move had been the wrong one. Without delay he acquired a house at Craymere Beck.

My brother and I knew very little of this at the time, only the forthcoming coming adventure was imminent.

The day duly arrived. Father was loading up the cart; he had made previously, a fine cart with wheels from a Motor cycle or small Car. All of our worldly possessions in turn, placed in the cart, surmounted with the large tin bath. Mother seeing to the remainder of smaller Items in the house and as one may guess, making sure the house was left clean.

My brother and I, apprehensively following Father and the Cart up the loke onto the road, the load runs well over the tared surface, the Crossing Gates being open to the road, Father was able to make a run up the slight incline on to the metals and over to the Craymere road.

Some of the load became dislodged at that moment, and adjustments made to the load as we encountered the unmade track to Craymere. This road had only been repaired where large pot holes had been made by many horses drawn carts. The stone from the heaps by the road side bound together with the marl, made very little improvement over the pot holes.

Father having to compete with this and two lad's intent on seeing how far they may run making the dry earth rise in clouds of dust. Demanding us to stop or we would be in serious trouble. Resolve to the journey; we ran on the grass strip that was between the cart ruts, in serious discussion as to why it was so. Decided it was to keep the Horses feet clean and delighted in explaining it all to Father. He was not amused and again demanded we keep up with him or get lost forever.

At last we come to the incline running down to Craymere and the Beck. The water was well up the road; each side, the small bridge only wide enough for a person on foot, the bottom of the ford being stones and loose rubble gave Father quite a challenge to make it through. My Brother and I became quite wet. Small boys and water do not mix very well.
Making it to the other side with relief. Father with re-found energy takes the rise in the road up to the Craymere beck cottages. Our house was to be; the very last one in the row. A large Farm house having; at one time been the Village Shop of Mr Fox.

Mother had been previously with father and some preparation had been made for our arrival, it was not long before my brother and I were tucked up in bed, all so very strange but with the excitement of the day soon asleep.

A new day dawns, a large room, a new house, so much to explore, hardly time to eat our bread and milk before wanting to go and see it all. Our breakfast was bread cut up into small squares covered with goats' milk and a sprinkling of sugar. Our grand Father had goats and saw that we had plenty of milk. Father said, "Now we shall have our own goat someday".

It was not long before we found the small shop. A door leading from one of the rooms, and one on to the road for customers. It was small inside, a counter and shelves; lined with the names of many Items that would have been for sale. It was not long before the doors to the shop were locked. I expect Father thought it was for the best. However, there were many other places to investigate.

Out the back once having been the Dairy, a long-whitewashed building, with slabs to place the products, it was very cool in there. I remember the smell of whitewash and damp. A smell, that brings back a longing for the old days, cold and bleak as they were. Held the romance of times gone by.

One forgets the hard ships encountered on the way.

Two large rooms on the ground floor, one with a small window looking up the garden road towards "Burnt house". The farm house on the road to Thurning. Upstairs, two large rooms, our room was on the end, also with a small window looking up the garden road.
I expect mother realised my longing; to be able to look over the fields. Sometimes after we had retired for the night, father would have to rush upstairs to see what the commotion was all about.

The bed had desired to try to get to the room below, Father would find us in our bed at an acute angle, like a ship on a rough sea, the leg having gone through the floor.

This had obviously been a regular occurrence by the number of tin plate patches on the bedroom floor.

Mother one day decided to paper our bed room, there were off cuts from the rolls of wall paper, these my brother and I, filled Fathers cycling gloves with, making boxing gloves; enacting the forth coming big fight between, Tomy Farr, and Joe louis, that we had heard the men talking about.

Mother engaged in her task decided it would be a good Idea for us to go over the road into the field, where, Mr Brownsell was cutting his large field of corn. For a treat we may take some of the Masons Ginger Beer she had made. Peace prevailed in the work place for some time, our return became overdue and later rescued from our slumbers from one of the corn stooks.

Since in more enlightened years. Home-made Ginger Beer has been found to have at least; seven percent Alcohol.

Father is now a member of the Hindolveston silver band, he brings home the Big Bass Drum, after a while this mysteriously disappears. I could see no reason for that; it was great fun.

However, like all good things they decay, the poor old house is forsaken for one further down the row, the second one up from the end. A Mrs Partridge had Died, and we were to live there. Maybe the rent was less than the large house.

A new home and many things to explore. Mother and Father had previously spent some time preparing the cottage for the move. Our arrival was to a nice comfortable room with a nice warm fire going in the grate, we sat on the Peggy rug for a while out of the way. Mother had many things to do.

The Impetuosity of two boys soon become a tour of discovery. The back door is somewhat higher than the other cottages in the row, two steps needed to step up from the yard. The door opens on to a small room "The kitchen", a window by the door looking out into the yard, the wall adjoining the first house in the row. A Mr and Mrs Partridge.

In the right corner, the copper for washing, a small grate below to heat the water, all the water needed to be fetched from the well in the yard, "though for washing", Mother would use the rain water when it was available, in the centre a grate with two very small hobs either side, mainly for cooking and boiling the kettle. Mother called it the old muck dropper, for its habitually scattering ash to the floor, whenever it needed attending to.

In the left corner the wall Oven, two shiny brass knobs above its door for moving the soot rake over the oven, another brass knob on the door itself, below another grate to heat the oven, all the grate's emerged into one chimney, and shared by the adjoining cottage.

At times when the fire in the oven or copper would not go very well, or as Mother often said, "would Not draw".
She takes a small sack well damped in water, with her back to the offending grate, and whack it through her legs dislodging hopefully the offending soot.

Directly opposite the back door another steps up to the door leading into the front room. To the left of the kitchen directly by the back door, the door to the stairs and the bed room's. About eight stairs that rose up in a ninety-degree turn, to the landing that was open to the small bedroom.

Also, below the stairway a small room for garments and boots that one may need, or the odd rabbit. !Dead of course. Some of the cottages' used it for the coal. Father was to have our coal in one of the sheds that went with the cottage.

The front room up the step; much larger, only to be used for "High days and Holidays". A quotation often used. This room had a window looking out on to a small garden bordering the road to Burnt house. Opposite, The drying ground. A large Area of grass, a large walnut tree and a rising bank up to Mr Brownsels field. All the cottage's may use it for their linen to dry, or whatever they chose. Father later tethered our Goat's there. Also, a door into the front garden that was seldom used.

The wall to the left, adjoining, Mr and Mrs Smith. they had one son Donald; about our age. Two cupboards with a fireplace centre, another muck dropper with two small hobs either side. The chimney served booth cottages, often the next door's cooking smell would waft through.

Upstairs two bed rooms. My brother and I shared the small room above the kitchen, it had one small window looking out into the yard, the stairway had a rail part way round the top.

Father had made a gate to prevent us from falling down the stairs. Not an uncommon thing to happen in those old cottages, the other bed room much larger a window overlooking the road. Mother and Father's room.

Out in the back yard each cottage had a strip of grass, and path leading up to the toilet and small shed, like most cottages the toilet, was placed well away from the house. Ours of course a touch of luxury. Not just a nail in the wall to hang the squares of paper, our one had a board

Father made, a hook to hold the string, having been threaded through the paper, a loop formed to hang on the hook, a small box at the base of the board, to hold the candle and matches.

Mother often would send one of us to find Father for his meal, and the smoke from his cigarette wafting over the top of the door gave him away; as he enjoyed a read from the newspaper squares. On more than one occasion, Father would return to the house. "Mother, those dam boys will burn that place down before long". Referring to my brother, or I, having set fire to the paper in the toilet pail. Sometimes it became rather full.

A task for Father to take the pail up to our garden, quite some walk, and no one would dream of doing that job until after dark.

It was not long before the steps by the back door were replaced with one large one. Father obviously had in mind building a porch over the door, to make the house warmer, and to keep various things in like an extra pail of water.

Father a carpenter by trade, completed his apprenticeship in the locomotive works at Melton Constable, in the boiler lagging department. This would be only one; of his many porches and sheds.
The piece of grass at the back was cleared and soon Father had a frame erected, covered it with chicken wire, followed by covering all with sacking, and a thick coat of tar and sand, he now had a cycle shed.
Tar was cheap, one may get five gallons from the gas works for sixpence.

My brother and I, played in and around the yard, Mother took us for walks around the lanes, looking for blackberries when in season, or loading the pram up with wood, found by the hedge row, we searched for the wild flowers as they came into season, and looked for birds' nests; seeing the one with, the most eggs in. The only eggs we took home were, Moor Hen or Pheasant, that was later after starting School.

I started School at Five years old. Well not on the first day of the week, Mother could not remove me from under the couch in the front room. Here I took cover when it was announced that, I would be going to School that day. I had been previously well briefed of the fact, and was able to make my refuge, and remained firm until Father came home, and helped me out with his boot, later to "Regret the action". Mother said years later.

I was eventually taken by Mother next day, well dragged I should say. To the Infants class at Briston Primary Church School. Howling all the way, a Miss Williamson the teacher, sat me in a blessed rocking Duck, not that it was any help; the rocking Horse; vacant at the time may have quelled my tears. later I was given a slate and chalk. The exercise book and pen would come later when I had learnt my ABC and times table's. Mother took me for a week, then I made my own way from Craymere to the School, joining in with others on the way.

Father was now working for the Coop at Melton Constable, his main job was on the Coal round, though he had to do the groceries, or bread, should one of the other men be away,

No extra pay, they had a flat wage, and the hours were, until the rounds were done. Sometimes he would be on the coal all day then have to clean up and help with the other deliveries. The wage was about One pound ten shilling a week . Father often brought the coal lorry home. Mother quickly sweeping off any loose pieces of coal and the dust for our fire, !They waisted nothing.

Though not six years old, often I would sit in the lorry, visualising how it all worked, and at that early age, I remember having worked out the transmission. Having rode in the lorry at times in the yard, and watched Father manipulate the gears. I arrived at the conclusion that the engine turned the gearbox, the gearbox turned the shaft to the rear axle, and the wheels. I could not visualise the clutch, I thought the peddle separated the gears somehow in the gearbox.

I often wondered if this ability to decipher a situation, was anything to do with the meaning Mother spoke of when relating to My birth time. "During chime hours".

Father had lately been leaving the coal lorry on one of Mr Emersons fields, behind the large barn. On this particular morning I decided to give him a surprise, he was not to impressed at the time.

Early before Father was ready to collect the lorry, I was in the cab moving all the relevant control's in an endeavour to get it going before he arrived, his approach hampered by my hasty retreat to my refuge, I bolted the door paper and candle for company.

Father could not start the lorry either, no wonder I had been fiddling with the controls, and to have the choke or ignition in any other than the correct position was fatal, it would never start. "Mother where is that dam boy" he has been fiddling with the lorry, now it will not start. They tracked me down to my refuge. "Just tell me what you have done", he said, in tones that did not register anything other than the slipper across my backside. I remained firm, all was quiet for some time, the sound of the lorry going away, brought me out into the yard.

It was just a matter of time, keeping out of Fathers way for a few days. Not so difficult we were always put to bed early and Father often home late.

I had previously taken the handbrake off, when the lorry was in the yard, it rolled back into the hedge luckily, and not down the road into the water. None of this added to Fathers love of me at the time, the Coop certainly would not have been very pleased, to have had to rescue the lorry, as it should have been taken back to the depot not left at Craymere.

One day the lorry stopped in the yard, the back loaded up with wood of all shapes, it was unloaded into the Drying ground. Some of the cottage's had chicken runs in there, as well as drying the clothes it was near to the house an overflow from the gardens.

We! were to have a Goat. The hut was erected, two stakes put into the ground a wire stretched between them that the goat may run tethered between.

I was brought up on goats' milk from my Grand Fathers goat's, also my brother. In fact we were all brought up on it, with the exception of Peter called Dick, another thing about our family, not one of us were called by the names we were christened with, for some reason or other, and later given a nick name; that, for some people stuck.

I for instance James called Peter because that is what my Grand Father wanted in the first place; David John called Tubby. Kenith called Hinny. and Peter called Dick. To please one of my Mothers brothers.

I later became Granfa, no doubt because of the hand me down clothes, I wore at School. Though Mother done her best to make them fit, and in the cold weather, An Army great coat and man's cap done little to my appearance. I will say, while there were just my brother and I, we were dressed very well. Leggings Blazer and Jacky Cogan cap, we always had some new clothes for the Chapel Anniversary, and last year's best; for School. To be taken off as soon as we arrived home.

Dick the youngest of the family, was not expected to survive but a few weeks, the goat milk he would not keep down. Mother tried many things; pity old great grandfather Jackson was not still with us he would have known what to do. More about him later, the Doctor called at great expense, it was six pence to get the Doctor out, he declared that it was only a matter of time before we lost him. Mother told Mrs smith next door. "Have you tried Nestles milk she said". "That in the tin". Mother remarked, "we can't afford that". However, with reluctance, Father got some from the Coop and the change was remarkable, he started to do as the old folks say. Put on flesh and no looking back.

The back of mothers groceries books always had a little that could not be paid immediately, this extra cost done little to eliminate the ever "Increasing bill, she remarked, "without ever begrudging a penny"
That it took ages to get back to a level keel. Times were hard yet they asked nothing from no one.   Not that others were any better off anyway.
Our Breakfast was mostly bread and milk, squares of bread cut up and covered with goat's milk, sometimes a sprinkling of sugar.
My grand Father his breakfast mainly of Tea Sop, Bread with tea poured over it, the remainder of the tea, with milk and sugar before going to work.

They were considered to be Middle Class.
Nanny arrived after we had gone to bed, my brother and I hurried out into the drying ground. Under the Walnut tree, "A Goat". Light cream and some brown on her coat, no horns, we had expected our goat to have horns.

One of our tasks to be, with the hand cart to gather grass from the roadside, as the grass became plentiful the Goats were staked by the road side. Father saw to that before he left for work, Mother had the job of getting them home again. There were always some titbits in the hut for when they arrived back home, often mother struggling to hold the chain; two lads running with glee by her side, trying to keep up. She has to release the chain, and off they go chain ringing and bouncing along the road, not to arrive before they had eaten all the titbits, would prove fatal, they would be off again. Goats can be such fun.

Rocket had arrived, now we had two goats. Rocket was very thin, Father hung his hat on her protruding bone's while he milked her, he said she will fatten up. I never saw much change in her condition though she seemed happy enough. One day they had to have a drench for some reason, we were very concerned.
Father said it will be all right and will do them good. From a shelf in the kitchen, a bottle filled with a mixture, Mother helped as Father pored the mixture into the goat's throat, also on the shelf was some black treacle and sulphur, this also for the goats. At times in the winter we had some as well
"Sulphur and treacle are very good for you" Father said, though it did make one fart very smelly, rabbit seem to do that also, so I suppose they are very good to.
Father a man always trying to improve things, by now we had a sink in the back kitchen, built up on bricks and a pail below to take the water, care had to be taken not to let it overfill. This being reasonably clean the water may be thrown out onto the grass at the back. I do not think any of the other cottages had a sink, all there washing would be done on the kitchen table. Bathing was in the tin bath in front of the kitchen fire. Saturday night usually reserved for this.

Lighting varied considerably between the cottages. At first, we had a two-burner oil lamp, opening the back door on a winter night was the cue to call out "Mind the lamp". The glass chimney was prone to crack with the inrush of cold air, quiet an expensive item, a candle was used for the other rooms and the bed rooms. Though in our bed room, we had a Kelly lamp, a small oil lamp with a round wick, the base containing the oil weighted so to keep it upright, if accidentally knocked over it would spring upright again. One day Father obtained a Mantle lamp, it had a round burner and could be adjusted to a blue flame that through the mantle gave a very bright light.
Father was proud of the new light, in fact after dark he asked my brother and I, to go up Ollys hill and see who had the best light. Reporting back, the first house, no light, our house a very bright light, next, Mrs Smith a moderate yellow light, next a little glow most likely a candle. Some no light at all, probably sitting by the fire light, and that is how it was in those days. It was the normal thing and accepted as natural.

In our bedroom the Kelly lamp stood on Fathers book case, the case containing all his chapel Prizes, this is where I saw the Apparition. I looked from under the bed clothes for some reason,

and before the bookcase, a lady looking towards the lamp hands held forward as though to warm them.
This scene I saw from time to time, and resulted in me repeating my first action, tucking back under the bed clothes and pretending to be asleep. To me the lady was young not old. later I was to here talk of a ghost presuming to be old lady Partridge. I had decided the lady was someone other than Old lady Partridge.

Mother who when questioned about the Ghost by a neighbour, made light of it saying, "Oh yes he follows me up at night and down again in the morning". This confused me to some degree, my nights were not always happy ones. I had many nightmares in those early days. Sometimes I was guilty of misbehaving, mother would say. "God puts it all down in his book", none of this helped very much. I of course did see the Apparition, and later I will give the proof in a twist to this tale.

Like all boys I gave my parents a few frights. I had committed some misdemeanour and made for my refuge, up the Oak tree down the Burnt house road. It had four large branches forking out at the top, no one could find you there. As it was getting dark Father and Mother came down the road calling. "It is all right do come home wherever you are", they had looked everywhere.

As they passed my refuge I slipped down and ran home. The presence of my boots by the door indicated the bird had come home to roost. I got away with it as usual.

There were not many children to play with in the row, the lad next door, he was not allowed to play with us, the two lads by the Beck, we were not to play with them, though we did. "They were very poor", Mother said, and had to take their boots off after School to save them, they went bare foot. We thought this grand and often in hot water for doing the same.

This we never had to do, though I will say we did spend rather a lot of time in wellies. We played in the Beck enacting things we had seen in second hand comics. Like panning for Gold and coming up with a few coppers mostly of the old cartwheel type.
Revellers from the Plough Inn Public house, I am sure were our benefactors, the crossing being unmade and very rutted, causing them to take an unsteady passage through the Beck.

My brother and I were now booth going to School, we walked the road and sometimes took the footpaths, also we had to attend Sunday School. The Methodist Chapel in Hall Street in the morning, Bible lessons and the main service.

In the afternoon Thurning Church, Scripture lessons at the Rectory, and afternoon service in the Church.

The School itself made sure we had added scripture. Miss Williamson gave us tuition in the scriptures, in her Farmhouse near the School, this we liked as her mother gave us nice cake and tea, sitting around an oil stove in their best room. Not to forget the Salvation army, Joy hour that I will relate to later.

It was about this time in my young years. My brother and I about to go and play in the yard. Incisive, it was about to rain and a strong wind. September weather. Three figures standing in the yard by the well, caused us some concern, there dress to say the least was shabby. A lady and gentleman and a small boy, looking no older than us, though I am to believe he would have been between eleven and twelve years old. We were not sure what to do, go in and tell Mother, or stay. Our curiosity causing us to stay watching as the trio called from house to house. Mother would not say their business. I will come back to this story later.

Mother done her best to turn us out well dressed especially for Sunday School. This she achieved through the local Pack men who called, there was Mr Edwards, Pack man from Briston, the Chapel Minister, also Mr Moulton, he owned the Drapery store in Holt.
For a few pence a week, Mother was able to send us once a year to the Chapel Anniversary admirably dressed.

This was the yearly Prize giving. One had to have so many attendances at the Chapel Sunday School to qualify to take part, this was indicated on a small card. John Claxton slightly senior in age was given the honour, we found that a poppy head in season would be the ideal substitute for his stamp. We were mainly thinking of the trip to the seaside that was part of the deal. Each child had to learn some poetry that needed to be recited on the day, the prize was then given to each participant, this was not one of my favourite occasions.

My uncles who on occasions visited us tried their very best to teach us more colourful verse about, "Two old Crows. I am sure Mother half expected our recitation to deviate from its original path.

On the Sunday afternoon, in the company of the two boy Hannents William and Jack we walked up the Burnt house road to the Perts, they lived in one of Mr Brownsels cottages near Manor Farm, together all walked to the rectory at Thurning, for more Bible classes. The rector at the time, Mr Miller. Again, were marched down to the Church for the afternoon service, before going back home to tea.

Another string to our Bow of Religious education, was the Salvation Army. The Salvation Army Hall, called the Army Barracks, was down Church lane by the new post office. I remember the pillars supporting the roof, the large pot-bellied stove, warm and inviting after a walk from Craymere, on a cold winter night. It was Joy hour, the Captain played a guitar on the stage, some joined in, he told stories. Some nights Baked potatoes were available, or a cup of peas. We seldom had a penny to pay with. Mr Burt Reynolds, an Engine driver on the railway, was always there helping. A devote Salvation Army man, he provided our penny, and for others I am sure.

Other adventures out of the village. The Sunday School outing. With Mother on the day, a walk to the Chapel, we were told to keep looking on the road, in the dirt you may find a penny or two, and there sure enough a few pennies were found, and we had a copper or two to spend at the sea side, a stick of rock to take home I am sure.

The children, a whole day on the sands by the sea, guarded by parents in turn. Later in the day a feast was laid on in the Sheringham Chapel rooms.
More sand and then home in Parkers Bus from Hindolveston. It was a good thing finding those pennies on the way. Father would have been cross, spending money, housekeeping money on such things as rock. After all we had spent the day on the sand's

Not only the Chapel rewarded our efforts to attend regular. The Church gave a Christmas party for those attendants, sometimes in the Rectory or at, Rookery Farm. Mr Fisher he had two sons James and John; booth attended the Melton Constable secondary School as did we. Mr Fisher saw if it was good enough for the majority of the Parish, it was good enough for his son's. He was always ready to give praise or reward and liked by his workmen. One day I was out playing by the line near his land, the Train had set fire to his corn, I made an effort to beat out the flames, others arrived and I returned to our house, later to find Mr Fisher had come to the house to thank me personally for my efforts. He gave me sixpence, allot of money to a lad. At one of the party's at Rookery Farm I guessed the number of things in a jar, I was rewarded with a prize.
Was I proud of myself? It took very little to please us in those days, our lot was very small.

One particular Christmas party at the rectory I remember very well. Miss Lilian Partridge, she lived in our row also worked in the Rectory and helped in the Sunday School. She was also

required to help with the party and was to be our escort to the Rectory. The rector at the time, the Reverent Miller, our third brother on the way and Mother could not take us. The party progressed the games played the fare enjoyed. Until it came to the Christmas tree.
Every child had a gift of one description or another, my brother received a toy GUN, my eyes lit up in anticipation. I unwrapped my gift a toy motor car, the disappointment it must have been evident to all, the time to go home could not come fast enough, wrapped up in our coat's and scarf's trotting behind Miss Partridge, we turned the corner to Burnt house.
By now I was in no mode for any comforting banter, my brother swaggering with his GUN. We came to the hill at Burnt house, running trying to keep up I drooped the car, dashed after it and stood on it. "That was it", all the swear words my Uncles had paid me pennies to repeat, and some I had no Idea of, came flying out in a string of oaths to the car. Miss Lilian Partridge stood aghast staring at this evil being, in horror turned and ran off into the dark. Leaving my brother and I to find our own way home,
Not that it bothered us we had made that journey many times alone. There was no repercussion to the incident, I would expect, it may have been difficult for Miss Partridge to give an accurate description of the event to Mother.

School was a journey I was never fond of. At least the School part of it. Sometimes we took the footpath through Munns green, past the wash pits. The imagination running wild as one passed by the two ponds that made up the wash pits,
Sheep were washed there before going into the waiting pen by the old Factory . It was all part of the Wool trade of Norfolk. Wool transported on the back of the Sheep to Munns green. - Told to me by my elders. - "From different parts", penned off in nearby fields, washed then sheared.

The Wool then taken to the old Factory barn to await processing in the Factory building, the processed Wool returned to the barn for storage and dispatch.

On to Ridlands Bridge, no more steam trains rumble above, as one stands below. On to the recreation ground, over the road and on to the School green.

In May this was more exiting. The May Fair gave us a holiday, there were cattle for sale, and a grand Fair for three days. Rides, roundabout's, and swings, and lots of side shows. It was at times, like the May Fare, we wished home was near to the Village.

In the early days we referred to going to Briston as going to Town, also the fact that lunch times at School were rather long, my brother and I took our lunch in a bag over the shoulder, drink was a bottle of tea, cold by lunch time. There was no dining room, the lobby was left unlocked if it was cold or wet, if fine one may take one's lunch into the playground or the green. Our lunch varied from time to time.

Father was able to get Offal from the Butchery at the Estate, during his visits' there with his work. Deer was often on the menu, Deer tongue, Mother would make a stew, and we would have it in little brown bowls. Since then I often wondered how we managed to stop it from spilling,

I do remember bragging about having Deer for lunch. I say Lunch though a word we never used, in our household, it was dinner and tea.
Dinner was midday and tea at five, the only variation was during harvest time and tea became Foursy's.

Mr Godfrey had the Fish and Chip shop near to the Village green, there were occasions when Mother gave my brother and I, two pence to get some chips to go with the bread and butter we had in our lunch bag. A chance to try the delights of Ice cream, not that we had not, ice cream before.

A Mr Wakefield from Hindolveston, he came around with kippers he smoked himself, and renowned for their excellence. In the summer he came with Ice Cream, and served it into a cup or bowl, whatever one chose to take out to his cart.

We called it cold tater's, though I expect it was some kind of frozen Custard. With our two pence a visit to the chip shop. "Two Halfpenny worth of chips please Mr Godfrey, and may we have some batter scraps with them", a kind man though some did say he had a glass eye, that at times found its way into the fry, we could not hold that against him.
With the remaining penny, a call at the Post Office. Mr Stanley and Albert Howe, "Ice cream please Mr Howe", could your half it and put half in each cornet please, oh dear; you boys will take all my profits.   We saw none of his profits and left saying. "We did not want any of those anyway" .

I suppose a lesson here somewhere, not to use words to children that have no immediate meaning.

Sometimes on the way to School, I would set Eel lines in stone Beck. The best I caught was one foot and two inches long. Aurther Willimot said. "It was a good Eel for the Beck", it was taken home and cooked. Like all the things we caught fishing or by any other means. What is the point of fishing if they are not for eating? The Gos pit was another of the places we fished for Roach, and only the very small ones put back.

These adventures often made us late home from School, we were not very popular for that.

Our life at Craymere was very pleasant, my other two brothers had arrived now, and with the four of us it must have been quite a hand full for Mother, she still had time to take us on walks with the pram to look for the first primrose and wild Violet, gather Hog weed for the rabbits, and any loose wood that may be in the hedge row for the fire. Returning back home from our walks, down Olly's hill, I can still see over the drying ground to the bog, under the large Walnut tree lay the two goats, waiting to be milked.

Mrs Smith walks over the road with a pail of slops, to be thrown with a swish on to the bank bordering the drying ground. No drains here. The Electricity has not come yet, it will take another twenty years before the switch replace the candle holder, at Craymere Beck.

A well-known photographer, Mr Remington took a photograph looking out over the Bog and Mr Wacters Farm, in the early nineteen hundred. It shows the Marsh land piece, we call the Bog. Children playing, I expect it was well drained then, and over towards the Farm, the gardens running up to the house in the distance.

Sitting on the rail of the foot bridge. Teddy Massingham, attending their Cows. Teddy then only a lad, he would have walked them down from the Farm at the old Factory turn, feeding off the roadside grasses as they walked, a drink at the Beck and home again for milking.

It was all over grown when we played there, part of its Marsh land. Though the garden still had in its apple and a cherry tree, growing in the hedge that divided the Bog and garden, many games we played there. I was enthralled by the Novel. Tom Sawyer, and imagined his adventures in our play.

I had become familiar with the Bog, that extended beyond the hedge, and over to the lower part of the Common. I could cross over to the other side without sinking into the Mire, no one could catch you there unless they knew the path's through.

The common covered with Heather Gorse and Broom, the bracken so high it may be pulled over and made into fine dens. On the odd occasion a grown-up who thought we had no right to be there, came after us. We took flight over the Bog, a refuge in its own

Our home at Craymere

Cowboys and Indians; another game. This did not develop fully until the age of eleven after we had been to the village and seen our first Film. A Matinee, Buck Jones cowboy, followed by Alice in Wonderland.

On wet days we played bus drivers and conductors on the stairs, one giving out the tickets to the pretend passengers the other driving.

We had once been to Grimsby with our parents and seen the Trams and Buses. I do not count Birds nesting, though this was only to claim the nest with the most eggs in, unless it was a Moorhen, or larger bird that could be taken home for tea.

On the Bog, we made. Bows from the willow, arrows from the reed, tipped by a small piece of Elder sharpened to a point, and see how far the arrow could be fired. These games by the way were seasonal.

Pop guns we made from a suitable piece of Elder, the pith pushed out, and if the bore was too small for the Acorn now in season, a poker made red hot in the fire was used to enlarge the bore. Carefully avoiding Mother in the proses, though not always successful, the Plonker made from Hazel, shaped to a handle, and the rod shaven down to fit the Bore,
The tow on the end of the rod, formed by plenty of spit and banging on a brick wall, until the fibres in the wood turned back making a mop head.
With an Acorn in one end thumped firmly into place with the handle end of the plonker, plenty of spit down the barrel, a quick blow into the barrel to increase the air volume, rapidly insert the tow of the plonker, and ready to fire. The handle of the plonker pressed to one's middle, hands grasping the Barrel and pull, resulting with a resounding bang and fast disappearing Acorn.

Of course, two Acorns one at each end, and you have a twicer, two bangs with one loading.

Staying with guns, we cut a piece of hazel about six inches long, made a slit about three inches down the stick, and with one's knife in the slit but the sharp blade facing the other way, one was able to cut a taper in the slit. This was a Haw gun. The haw from the Hawthorn hedge placed in the slot, the stick squeezed, and out fly the haw, if the haw was well ripe it worked very well.

Another Haw gun was made again from Elder. A suitable piece about six inches long, the pith pushed out, a slit cut about two inches from each end, this portion in the centre cut out looking something like a boat, into this centre a spring was fitted. The best spring came from a ladies Corsets, we found them in the pit holes, (waste tip). The spring about seven inches long, one end pushed into the formed part and up one end, the remainder of the spring bent into an arc. By pushing more or less spring into the first end and bending accordingly, one could get the spring to remain under tension, touching its other end.

The game was to fire from the boat shaped chamber a Haw, having placed the Haw in position one's finger through the spring loop and pull, the spring fires the Haw out the end.
Catapults everyone made a catapult, usually from an old cycle tube.

We ran hoop's, though to find a cycle tyre was not easy. The grown-ups who had cycles, recycled old tyres by cutting out the wire from the rim and putting two tyres on one wheel, moving them round so the good part covered the bad.

Tip cat. The cat was a piece of stick tapered at each end, one had a stick to hit the cat on the taper, as it flew into the air it was hit again to see how far one could hit it.

We had tops and whips, though not much use until one got on to the tared road in the Village, there one could keep hitting the top and spin it down the road. The best top was the little dolly, not the tubby, the tubby spun longer, but the dolly, a narrow body with a large head; caught with the whip from low down, would come up off the road, and fly for many yards and land still spinning. The game again to get as far as one could without the top stopping.

We played flick cards at school in the playground, any man saw coming out of the little village shop with a packet of cigarettes was bound to be asked. "Can I have your Fag card please mister" .

When the Dew was on the grass a slide was started, and in turn tried to see who could make it longer I remember this being very popular.

Our road home, part of it was unmade. Meaning it was only earth. To repair any pot holes in the road stone and marl was placed by the side of the road, from these heaps of marl, we selected some of the better pieces took them home, crushed them to a powder, with a little water rolled them into Marbles. After drying in the ashes of the fire overnight, were quite respectable Marbles.
Though the cause of more than one dispute. If the win in a game of Marbles contained a glass ally, these came from within the neck of the bottle containing fizzy pop. Something we only heard about.

We made whistles from Cow parsley, we made pipes from our old friend the Elder. The stem from Honey suckle from the hedgerow, it is hollow. Mugwort after it has dried in the sun, we used as tobacco in our Elder pipes. lit by the Sun through the lens from an old Carbide cycle lamp.

We climbed trees. The most well-known was the hollow Oak, near the School green. "Out of bounds" said the School Master, a good reason for climbing it. One lad became stuck, his parents were informed, and the Father said. "Let him stay there until I have had my tea", even some of the girls climbed through its hollow trunk, and out along the lower branch to the ground.

Briston Fair. Way before the opening of the Briston National School, the folk of the Village and surrounding Villages. Would have indulged in the delights and pleasures of the Briston Fair. Many only to look, money for trivialities was just not available.

Recollections of we, now older pupils of Briston School, would have rejoiced and been delighted like me, not to have to attend School from the Thursday until the following Monday.

Thursday and Friday the School Green was the Auction ground, all relevant detail's concerning the Stock, may be seen on the Gable end of the Blacksmith Shop, partly covering older Notices.

The First big Sale, and Fair of the year.
"The May Fair". The Green full of Cattle and various livestock, having been driven from as far away as Binham by my Uncle, some from even much further.
Sometime pens were way behind the School, taking practically all the Green.

On the Mill road side of the Green, the Show men and their various rides, side shows, and entertainment's, some names I remember were. Kenny Gray. Underwood. (Rhubarb) pronounced Rubub and Mrs Gissie.

All will be on Parish records having paid the ground Dues collected by the Parish Clerk on arrival .

Always a Cheap-Jack selling Crockery, he would clash his wares together giving the impression of wares to last a lifetime as he repeatedly remarked.

The first Impression was the roar of the generators supplying the Electricity for the rides and colour full Decorations. For some of us this was the first time we had seen Electricity.

One was greeted by the Flare of the Cake Walk, with its two opposing decorated Walk ways, supported on cranks, that on-going round and round, would not only lift the Walk up and down, but backwards and forwards. The approach was up a sloping walk way, that also moved backwards and forwards. On paying one's penny at the Pay box, walking up the moving walk way. Then attempted. Those lucky enough to have a girlfriend may try to dance up into the walk Way, and along to the end under the colour full lights, and the Organ Music. That

Mysteriously came from a pile of unfolding Cards going into the Organ, Set in the centre of the whole colour full array.
A few steps along a stationary Walk, one again attempted the return journey trying not to fall over, great fun was had by all.

I actually tried it in 1950 on my demobilisation from the RAF. Having just enjoyed Fish and Chips beforehand, was I glad to get off? .
The next attraction the Roundabout's. The Steam Horses. A wonderfully Decorated and Illuminated Ride. Large Horses in pairs, not only going around and up and down, but the whole table modulated as they spun round, the lights and blurring faces of watchers below, a spectacle of wonderment.

Intermingled with the sounds of the rides, and motion of the Steam Engine, a combination of experiences one may never repeat.

The Dogem cars another spectacular, the attendants leaping from Car to Car, holding on to the pole at the rear, that conveying the Electricity to the car.
Its contacts showering sparks as the cars Bumped each other, this, the means of collecting Fares. Surprisingly no one seemed to get hurt.

A claxton horn sounded for the start and end of each ride, operated by a face in the Box calling for the Cars to go only one-way round, though no one seemed to be taking little notice, and I expect even less after the public houses had closed for the night.

Further on away from the Bumpers. The Large swinging Boats gaily decorated, holding many passengers, given momentum by the attendant, the long ropes hanging from the gantry above, enabling the passengers to maintain momentum until such time the ride ended. The attendant then lifted up a long plank to rub on the bottom of the ride, bringing it to a halt.

The other side of the Fair. It being divided with rides to one side and stalls and side shows the other.

The stalls and games of skill varying from Dart boards, Rifle ranges, Roll a penny, with various prizes. Up to the Coconut Shy, where one may win a Coconut by throwing a wooden ball, dislodging the nut from its well-placed perch, on a handful of sawdust. The attendant who would sometimes adjust the sawdust to make the nut fall for a participant, who had tried with no success for many times.

There was much sawdust on the grass. lucky for us children, it contained many a treasure to be found after all was cleared and gone.

At the time water squirts . A lead tube filled with water that may be squirted at Girl or Boy friend, those we found and refilled.

Briston fair

The strong young men may show off, on the try your strength machine. A tall apparatus with a bell at the top, and graduations for those not able to make the striker hit the bell. By hitting a large wood pin in the base sending the striker up to the bell.

Mrs Gissie made the Rock. A must for all to take home, especially the Humbug Rock. My Mothers favourite.

As Children on a Saturday afternoon before the fair started, we would watch Mrs Gissie making the Rock, all different colours laid out in long strips on the large table, above a rail; where she

threw the colour full strips of sticky Rock, needed to be twisted together. Many times, she spit on her hands to enable the Rock to be formed as she wanted it.

Next to the Rock stall, an old cast Iron Copper, boiling away with scalding Fat. Spontaneously giving a roar not unlike the Sea striking the stones on the beach, as a large quantity of Chipped potatoes were thrown in. Either the smell, or the quality of the chips soon had Folk clambering for them.

Not many Children had the pleasure of the Fair, a few may be taken by their parents, but mainly as I remember. For the Grown-ups.

Our turn came hunting through the saw dust for wooden balls, left from the Coconut Shy. With luck a whole one may be found, or even a penny to spend at Mrs Cobles little sweet shop. The discarded led tubes having once been water squirts, the odd Dart flight, a whole dart a prize indeed. Empty Cigarette packet's where one may find a picture card, in the excitement of it all the owner discards the card with the empty packet.

Briston Fair in the Thirties, Quite something. Most of the Showmen household names.

One comment I heard as a young lad living in a row of semi-detached houses, has stayed with me over the years. Husband to wife. "I will be glad when the Fair come again, I am sick of scraping this butter off the paper. "I will win another Butter Dish" .

It was not all play. At weekend's and during the holidays, I often looked after cows feeding on the fields at Ridlands, behind the keepers' cottages, I think a Mr Barnes was keeper there then.

One had to meet the cows after morning milking at the Ridlands Barns, walk them up to the field about a mile, then stay with them to make sure they came to no harm. A nine-year-old boy with twenty cows to look after for one shilling a day. I am sure it was not for the money.

Most of the fence was broken down, and one ran from fence to fence most of the day and was glad when it was time to take them back for milking.

Later the Mechanics took over the farm "The Mechanised Farmers". They had tractors and worked at night with lights. A revelation in farming was beginning, large combines, not self-propelled as now. A converted thrashing drum pulled by the tractor.
Sometimes a horse was needed to help when the going was bad, the weather was not always kind, the corn not dry for the combine, so the old practice of cut shock dry stack, and thrash in the spring.

One harvest I rode a trace horse on that farm, the trace horse was to help the loaded carts to move over to the stack, a lad riding on the wagon horse, had to call out hold gee, before the wagon moved to the next shock for loading, as the load was getting high a fall from the top of the load could have been fatal. The chains of the trace cut into one's legs. It was not one of the better harvest jobs, not that I can ever remember getting paid. I was glad to be finished with that.

Easter Sunday was new clothes day, and in what our Mother could afford we paraded into Chapel. Last years old clothes now for school, and school clothes as they were, for after school and weekends.

Breakfast on the Sunday was an egg. I can't remember father having chickens at Craymere, though we did have a bird to fatten up for Christmas on house hold scraps. We also had other birds in small huts up in the top garden. The huts were Yew traps the birds were game. Father made them. Four hazel rods forming the base, a square with four more hazel rods from each corner, converging at the top in a point, the four triangular sides woven with Yew canes. Inside a suitable hazel rod, the two ends affixed to the rear triangle at the base, forming a half circle, just behind the front triangle at the base.

To set the trap, it was lifted up about six inches, a forked stick in the ground, there rested another short stick, passing under the base at the front, and resting on the half circle spring holding the yew trap up. A little corn sprinkled within encouraging the game to enter.
It would be normal for the bird to sit on the spring to Perch, triggering the spring allowing the whole trap to fall.

If mother saw one contained a catch, it was covered with a sack until father came home, I expect he had quite a few poached games, as I much later on.

At Easter We had a Chocolate egg also as I recall, they were poor yet managed to keep us up with other children. Going back to school children could be very cruel with their remarks about, what they had, and others did not.

Father tried to keep up with the times, we had a radio, not many radios at Craymere Beck. Possibly the only one in the row, the high-tension battery cost twelve shillings, the grid bias nine pence, with care may last nine months, the accumulator required charging each week. Mr Parker, he delivered the charged one each week, that cost sixpence.

I cannot understand why father could not have charged it on the coal lorry. We listened to, In Town to Night, a serial with Jock and Snowy, this was the night we were aloud up until seven thirty. Bath night. The bath before the fire and sometimes Father would bring home a double six chocolate bar to be shared. I do remember on the radio, Scot of the Antarctic, Mother turned it off at the story of the expedition ending, not for young ears. Take a look at TV today .

Staying with Easter. Lassie, my mother's sister, was staying with us. I expect for the birth of either Kenny or Dick. She met with Alfred Barwick, a cousin on my grandmothers' side, he bought her a very large Easter Egg, as big as a football, all covered with candy flowers, and goodies inside. It was for safe keeping in Fathers gramophone cabinet. One day a Shriek, and loud threatening cries, as to our forth coming fate.
Poor Aunt Lassie, she had turned around the egg, her lovely Easter egg, only to find the whole of the rear gone and the goodies.

It started with just a small piece of candy from round the back of the egg, then a small hole was made, a few goodies, a piece of chocolate, and so on. In time I expect the lot would have gone. I am sure she saw the funny side later when she calmed down.

Father Valentine was also looked forward to. On that night we sat by the door singing. Old father valentine, God bless the baker, you be the giver, I will be the Taker. Now there should be a knock at the door, but no.

Mother said, "He will not come until your father gets home so he can have his valentine". After one song many songs later, a knock at the door, it was opened quickly, a parcel, who is it for? and so on until we all had one. Usually some sweets or a little toy. One year I got a pocket knife, the high light of the year.

But Christmas the family celebration, the run up to Christmas with plenty of warnings of who father Christmas would not be calling on, if they were not good. Letters up the chimney to father Christmas. I am sure they dropped down again into next doors fire. The two fire places were to one chimney, you could smell what they were cooking from our side often.
When we went to bed the house was as usual, sometimes the tree by the door, another time that had to wait for Father to come home, to go over to the wood and cut one. A glass of wine and some cakes left on the table for Father Christmas, he had the trimming up to do.

In the morning we find presents at the foot of the bed, and down stairs a large fire going. The tree all trimmed with sugar mice hung by their tails, and other goodies.

The room was all hung with trimmings. A pork pie with an egg inside, something they always had at Mothers home, when she was young, also to keep the worms from gnawing until dinner time.

We always had a good Christmas dinner, no one left the house, only to go over the yard; until the day after Boxing day. Our presents varied. One year we had a little boat that sailed round in water, it worked by heating a small boiler in it, two pipes out at the back, one drawing in the water one blowing it out causing the boat to move round a light house, that with a candle causing a vain to turn round, and light and shadows to be cast on the water.

Craymere mill

Another time an air ship that hung from the beams, when wound up the propeller drives it round the room. Some Fret work tools from Hobbies of Dereham, mostly things to share.

One year we both had peddle cars. Mother told Father; that Uncle Dick from London had sent the money for them.

Uncle Dick was in the Navy. But this was not the true story, she must have saved very hard to find the money for them. She did some spring cleaning at times for people. And one time was paid in kind. A three-burner oil stove, with large stand, an oil bottle at one end and a large oven at the other end . It was her pride and joy, and it gleamed from endless polishing.

We had the cars but a few days, when Uncle Jack from Blakeney came to visit. They had a large family. Mother had told of Uncle Dick paying for the cars, and being the old softy, she was, gave the racing car to Jack for his family. Thinking; I suppose, Jack would wonder.
"How is it" they get things from my Brother Dick and not I. Who knows, it's all in the past now.

Uncle William always came from Binham before the twelve days of Christmas, or the Sunday nearest, for the taking down the trimmings, and the goodies off the tree. He always had his share, we had them back later in the year, we did not eat the mice for ages, we played with them until they were black, then ate them.

Some of the winters were very cold, an extra blanket on the bed, an old army great coat, sometimes the rug off the floor. we got into bed with our socks on, sometimes get undressed in bed, in the morning; pulled our clothes into the bed to get warm before putting them on. How we survived the cold at times, I hardly know.

Before I leave Craymere Beck, I must relate some of the antics we preformed or were involved in.

The wet land upstream of the Mill, caused by the Mill dam being blocked up, all grown over and wooded, the Ideal place for wild fowl to nest. I could make my way through the wooded area to find the nest, and take the Egg's, the water quite deep in places. Young boy's do not think of hidden dangers, I was quite happy there and often alone.

One day, I found the hatch in the Mill wall, opened it; and could see the remains of the large water wheel. It had been the largest water wheel in Norfolk until Mr Philips, who had a timber business, took it out for fire wood, I am to understand.

I climbed in and over the shaft, below was the wheel sluice from the dam, looking very deep. Crossing the shaft; I explored what was left of the old workings. looking back; it very well could have been the last of my adventures, one slip and no one would have ever found me.
Singing Carols was under the leadership of one Collin Whitered. We met at the Beck; the first call was at the Farmhouse of Mr Wacter. His Mother wanted us to go up to her bedroom, and sing. We were surprised to see for the first time someone so old. She was over Ninety years old, quite unnerving for one so young to encounter, she reached below her pillow; and gave us a coin. It was a farthing.

Mr Bond he was the Inn keeper at the Plough Inn, he had a field behind the house, and mostly it was planted with corn.

Like all corn fields at harvest they attracted little Boys, he was a kindly man and always made us welcome. He had a Sail cutter, one of the early reapers, the blade reciprocating as the modern machine's, driven by a large single wheel at the point of balance, so as to give traction to the wheel.

The table supported off the ground by a much lighter wheel, the sail came down from above the drivers head on to the standing corn, pressing it on to the blade where it was cut close to the ground, the sail now sweeping the corn over the table, to be left behind and gathered up by hand, then tied into shoves, by using some of the corn as a bond, this Mr Bond patiently showed us to do.

I am sure the work could have been done much quicker by himself alone. However, he was a kindly man.

After the corn dropped off the sail to the ground, the sail; or I should say one of them, there being at least four, then rose up and over the driver's head completing the circle. Quite an ingenuous contraption for its day.

My Uncle, brother to my Grandmother, lived on a small holding just before the Factory turn, his name was Alfred Barwick. Quite a large family of them.
Now down the Factory turn; living in the Factory cottages, that had once been the work rooms of the Factory, My uncle. Fred Jackson. Brother to my Grand Father. Also, three other families, Bussey, Dewing, and Craske.

Our Family. Old John was Born in Edgefield in 1831, at the 1871 Census was living in Hall Street Briston, in a cottage next to where in the 1920's lived a Mrs Bambridge. His wife Born in Glanford in 1831. They were of the same age. I know little more than that.

The family came to Briston about the Eighteen Fifty's lived in Hall Street. Later moved down to the Farm in Factory lane, not all of them were given the luxury of Schooling, though great cousin William; was given one of the Bibles mentioned in the Briston National School Rules. I expect he left School at about eleven years old, in eighteen sixty-nine. The girls, some of them staying longer, all keen to learn as evidence of their enthusiasm found within effects fortunately saved down the family.

Old John the daddy of them all. A vet by learning, and Sheep Dresser, later to move down to the Farm in Factory lane, from where he Farmed and practised.

He was responsible for the Invention of the Sheep Dip before it became Law, though; he never took out the Patent for it, some other done that, leaving him somewhat annoyed so I am to believe.

I would not be surprised if he was not responsible for the Wash pits at Munns green. Not only Animals were his Patients.

He made Laudanum out of Poppy's. A mother calling upon him saying "John the child will not Due". Meaning It would not take its milk, it would not rest, or stop Crying. He gave her a Potion he had in store, in a twist of paper. For a copper coin .
The old man was no Fool. Psychology was nothing new in his field. The Patients complaint would more than often pass in a few days.

For many Ailments he gave a Pill, duly rolled in flour and liberally dusted with Alum to give it the Bitter Pill taste.

In time the patient duly recovers, unaware he has taken Rabbit dirt off the Common, with no more medicinal value than a few herbs the Rabbit failed to Digest.

A patient worse for Ale. It has been known of the younger men in the old days, to work a Harvest and then spend every penny in the Ale house. To the extent of returning home to bed, and on getting undressed, finding a few more coppers in his pocket, get dressed again; and go back to the Ale house to consume the remaining.

In despair, he may Call to John for help, the old man listens to his plea, and inability to pay. Sympathetically old John would say . "If I help you must obey my every word". Giving the Patient a large pill, and a Gill of water to take it with. Repeating "You must also drink one gill three times a day for two weeks". The patient thinking, he can replace the water with Ale. However Old John continues. "Should a drop of Ale pass your lips within that time, I will not be responsible for what becomes of you". "A fate worse than death".
The water alone would have improved the Patient. The Pill; a large piece of soap, duly rolled in flour and bitter Alum, would have caused very little bother.
For some it was a complete Cure, others found help in Salvation and later became devoted to the Cause.

My uncle Fred was a good man; and always had time for us, later I often when on to has small holding looking for rabbit's.

Also, in the Factory cottages lived the Family of Craskes. Their story I will now relate as I have been putting together over the years.

The tale of Fredrick Craske.
Three desperate figures standing by the Well in the yard, gazing along the row of cottages at Craymere Beck. Watched by two lads, indecisive as what to do, stay in the yard or go into the house, and tell mother.

There inquisitive nature overcome the desire to run. The old lady and Gentleman, and small lad obviously no threat to them. Watched as the shabby trio, enquired from house to house, as to the possibility of being able to shelter; in one of the sheds or outhouses, in and around the yard and properties.
They had tried to find shelter, from where their belongings had been dumped, without Charity; by the side of the road at the junction of the lane. The Factory Turn.

To no avail, without hope they return to their property. It was the belief of most of the local parishioners that to give any aid to this Family the same fate would befall them also. Most of them rented Estate property.

There only crime, I can only assume was that; they had become in arrears with the rent. This of course would become due each Michaelmas. The 29Th September and not the better time of the year to find oneself without shelter.

The early thirties and Frederick about twelve years old, though difficult to judge an age at this time.
However, there return to their belongings did not go unnoticed, and giving them respectable time to themselves.
Mr Alfred Barwick my uncle, who rented a small holding nearby, also used the large piece of Common land adjacent. Approaching but not wanting to belittle them, asked what the trouble was. Though well informed as most villagers would be. Listened as Jack related the story.

Alfred a veteran of the first world War. Where he lost his leg, was not going to be told what he may or not do, village gossip or otherwise. Told Jack he may put his belongings on the Common and stay as long as he wishes.

There were on the Common two rubbish tips, from here they found cast off materials, the Gauze, Broom and Bracken in plenty, and soon had a reasonable shelter for the time being.

Going by each day to School. We often would see the old lady standing by the roadside, at times Frederick would be sitting on the grass. I often wondered why he was not at School; I can't remember seeing him there. Being dressed as he were.

As lads, we wore hand me downs, but at least they were altered to a reasonable fit, he may have been in the older class. However, I cannot see the Authority getting very excited by his lack of attendance.

Jack and Tinifa found means of keeping themselves in food as well as shelter. I doubt that he would have poached Game. The risk was great, and from words the old man related much later, indicated he was not in favour of going to prison.

The Parish had means of giving them parish relief. The sum of about ten new pence a week, also help with shelter. But I believe earlier Threats made for any well-wishing person's, hampered any such forthcoming.
Living in the make shift shelter for a time, and later a canvas covered cart seen by the shelter on our way to School. We were a little apprehensive in passing on our way to School, the old lady's appearance causing us concern.

Having once called there singing Carols. And rightly so being rapidly shown the road. I very much doubt she would have done us any harm.

One day it was recalled to me. A Lady of some means saw this little lad going through the space in the hedge; to the settlement, on making enquiries into their situation. Became a benefactor by the means of a purpose-built wooden Bungalow of some description. This must have made life without a doubt at least tolerable.
Frederick now about sixteen or seventeen years had gone into Holt, for whatever reason he obviously walked. I doubt he had a cycle, however at that time a cycle lamp was reported missing, this ragamuffin lad had been seen, and the finger pointed at him. In those days If the Policeman said, "You done that". Then you; the chief suspect, would be up before the local Magistrate.

Frederick standing before the Bench, pleading Innocent. The Magistrate seeing the lad's plight, obviously understanding the situation, and that the penalty would be three years in the Red House. A Borstal institution, remarked. "The best place for you my lad is in the Army".

Now this is the last place Frederick wanted to be. Humble as his home was, fearful as he was of the Courts, with their Blessing arrived at the Royal Norfolk's Barracks and became a Volunteer.

He came back to Briston someone said. And what a remarkable change. Smart and looking well.

In 1939. The start of World War two, the services of Frederick and his comrades were needed. They landed up in France taking up Defensive positions, with the Expeditionary force.

Various skirmishes taking place in May 1940. At the time his Battalion were in the area, Foret de Marchienna. On the 11Th May crossed into Belgium and came under heavy Air attack. Moving about the country as directed. His Company to stem the advancing enemy. Taking up positions on the Bethune Estares canal. Near Le Paradis.

On the 25Th the German Army trying to cross the Canal. There were heavy Casualties on both sides. On the night of the 25Th, the 2Nd Battalion preparing for the onslaught; that must come very soon. By morning they were under heavy fire from Tanks, and mortar fire, there were many causalities on both sides again.

Frederick is Presumed to have been killed 26 May 1940 Age 20 years .

A life given for a country who had refused him food and shelter .

The stubborn opposition of the Battalion holding them at bay. The Germans themselves said "They were up against an Elite Corp". It is assumed that the German Commander so infuriated by the resistance, that may have been the reason for the predetermined Massacre that took place at, Duries Farm near Le Paradis.
Operation Dynamo took place 26Th May, taking off British Troops at Dunkirk. That when complete saved some 337000 men, without the Resistance of Pte Crask and many like him. More lives would have been lost, there selfless Sacrifice, saved the lives of countless men, enabling them to reach Dunkirk.

It comes to the end of my tale. It has been with me in many formats for years, with help I hope I have reached an honest conclusion.

The old people, I can only assume received the news. I have very little memories of there later life, only the old lady Died at their Home. The old man continuing for some time, he could be seen sitting outside by the road, and was glad of a passing chat, the words I was to refer to later was. "Well lad, I don't mind Going to prison, only they lock the Doors at Night". I expect he never did.

Again, I can only presume he died as he had lived. Alone at the Factory Turn Corner to a pauper's grave ?

It seems fitting that year 2000 and the last Official Dunkirk Memorial coming to an end, that the story of Frederick came to its final chapter. Not only has it been a
toil of memorial pleasure. And the final research very Emotional. I am Honoured to have taken part in it.

I Acknowledge that without the following help I may have toiled much longer. See the man who missed the Massacre. Cyril Jolly, whose notes from his book I could follow the Company.

Frederick Edward John Craske N0 5773186 2Nd Bn Royal Norfolk Regiment. The lad whom the parish would not give crust of bread or shelter. Gave his life for them.

Our Grand Father Had Died. He was a Guard on the Railway, and was injured from time to time, during his work Shunting, quite a Hazardous task especially at night. This I under stood was one of the reasons for his death in 1934 age 60 years.

Mother gave us the news one morning. I would have been about seven years old and did not rely understand what it entailed. Though I do remember it was like the time one realises Father Christmas doesn't come down the chimney any more. But one still plays the part.

My Grand Mother again tries to persuade Father to go back to Briston. Though at the time he was indecisive and life at Craymere continues .

A little older, and able to help Mother with the Shopping. Many Items we get from Mrs Codlings little Shop, just past the Factory turn on the right, set back from the road, the house a converted Railway carriage, a small wooden structure at the end was the Shop. She sold most things folks wanted; they had a Daughter Betty.

She was a little Tyrant, and her main aim in life seem to be getting home from School just before us and telling her Mother we were nasty to her. We then had to run the gauntlet of Mrs Codlings anger, her Betty could do no wrong, though Mother had been to see her over this matter many times.

We also Shopped at the Coop in Melton Constable. The large shop of the week, we were allowed to Wheel Mothers Bicycle, to hang the bags of shopping on the handlebars. Though a high cycle we still managed to ride some of the way, one time we had eight rolls of wallpaper, Mother had ordered, that time walking unaided by the cycle. Taking short-cuts from the Railway bridge at Ridlands through Munns Green, to the Wash pits, and up by Ridlands Farm. Birds nesting passing the time, caused some of the paper to get torn, again Mother was not Amused.

A Mr Burges worked in the Coop, a small bag of sweets always found its way into the bag, really one of the encouraging reasons for, our eagerness to do the shopping. November was Divi pay out at the Coop, Mother would go with us for the shopping, her Divi number was 29418. I remember it well, the brought forward items on the back of the book paid for, and a little left to call at Mr Fishers shop, it was also a Chemist shop, he had the nick name of Chemical Bill. November the Fifth, Fireworks day, that is what this is all about, eager eyes with noses pressed to the glass of the display, already deciding what they would do. Imagination running wild as usual; fizzling out as a dying pin wheel, Mother is seen picking out those fairy fountain's, spinning wheels, sparklers, and so on. No bangers no rockets. They were put away in Fathers cupboard until the day, however that did not stop prying hands from getting them out; just for a look. I am sure by the time it came for Father to let them off for us, half of the powder had fallen into the bottom of the box.

We often called to see Uncle Fred down the Factory turn. Tom Busy, he was living there sweet on Cousin Alice. William Spencer, Aunts brother, moved out on to one of Uncle Fred's large pieces of land on the Briston road. He had acquired a Shepherds hut on wheels, and lived there, we visited often he had lots of very old Pistols and various things a boy loved to see, he was very kind, and always pleased to see us.
Later as I was older, he let me loan his number twelve shot gun, he said it had been a rifle from the Bore War. Also, on the land lived, in a small black hut, about six foot by eight-foot, Tom Bussey's Father, it seems many old men lived in small huts or half Railway Carriages those days.

The Whitreds lived nearby, in a similar situation, quite a large family. I only knew Colin really as a School friend.

Father had Acquired a box of Kippers, one of the things possible if one had connections with a railway Guard. They brought them up from Yarmouth, to sell on, between themselves, or get the family to sell them, this became our lot, my brother and I, calling door to door, one half pence a pair. Old Bussey wanted only one kipper, we had no change, my brother was held to ransom, while I returned from home with his farthing change. Such were things in our school days.

May 1936 I am nine years old, more talk about Moving to Briston, however nothing comes of it and life goes on. I am now in the older class, liking School even less. Though I want to learn, my queries about things I did not understand, go unanswered, reading my Chapel prizes over and over, outdated newspaper's Father brings home, the squares of paper on the string in the closet. Adventure story's, like Tom Sawyer, Uncle Tom's Cabin, take me into my world of never. I am becoming a loner; it suits me anyway.

A little excitement, the School Christmas Party. Always a large tree, trimmed with goodies. The benefactor, Either Mr Higinbottom from the Lawn. West end Briston, or Mr Rothamere from Stody Lodge. Father Christmas, mostly Mrs Cully, from the store next to the Chip Shop. A party enjoyed by all. We usually received a present from the tree, this year one lad anxious not to be left out, being in the vicinity of one large white mouse hanging from the tree. Took one large bite and ran away with its head clasped between his teeth, hastily pursued by Miss Brown, who Tally Who'd him to earth by Mrs Corbels Sweet shop. A fitting end, though I am sure Charlie was able to suck his way out of that one. I have been requested to remark here.
Robert Cushion says, "He was no relative of his". The Court Retires.

Without warning we are again on the move. Father has been persuaded by Grandmother to move up into the Cottage, in Hall Street. Mrs Ducker has gone, the slightly larger of the two cottages is to be our new home. Three average size rooms upstairs will make life less crowded, now there are four lads, My brother and I. Kenny. and Dick. names they take with them through life.
The house had only one door when we came, a living room with white washed beams, a small fire place, a hook above the fire to hang the pots and pans, two side hobs. The floor was pan tiles laid on sand, a cupboard to the left of the fire, to the right a door to the stair way, with eight steps up to the bedroom, a small bedroom to the right of the top of the stairs, a large room at the top and a long one just off it, to be for my brother and I.

Just off the living room a long kitchen, known as the back house, a pantry at one end, and a fire place at the other, one side of which was the wall oven. The space to the right had been the wash boiler. That now is in the wash house, the room below the small bed room.

Only one door into the house, the wash house had its own door outside, bathing on a cold night was not a long job, the water was heated in the wash copper, that had to be brought up from the well, that was down by my grandmother's house, or from the soft water tub outside, any more than two pails of water from the well, gran wanted to know what was being done with all that water.
Little did we know that in less than three years' time, life as ourselves, and everyone knew it, was to drastically change, and the country would be at war with Germany.
My grandmother lived in the house below, it had a large garden, a paddock, also a large meadow, where Jack the pony lived, at times he was brought up to the paddock. Grandmother worked hard, she got little help from her sons, they of course had their own lives to live.

She dug her garden, grew for her own needs, and for the pony. Even saved a little from her pension of ten shillings a week.

She brought up my sister as well, she had everything she wanted.

Father cultivated our garden, there were no greengrocers' shops in the village then. One man did come around the village, and surrounding villages, with a flat cart, sold fruit and veg. He came from Briningham, Sid Wright, and later took over the little sweet shop near the Village green. A Mrs Corbels "Polly". Owned it before him.

Father was still working for Latham and Co. Delivering all kinds of flour and cake mixes and breakfast foods from the Dept at Dereham. He had to cycle there to collect the van, sometimes he was able to bring the van home, if he was not far away from home. This job lasted until the outbreak of the war. He then worked in the waggon repair shops at Melton Constable.

As lads my brother and I, and the Hannents who still came to play. Followed our usual pursuits. Bird's nesting taking up much of the time at the moment. It was on one of these excursions I had my accident. Father had obtained two cycles for my brother and I and made them rideable. With our sticks grasped about the handle bars, over the Gate house and down the Craymere road to where the Boys Billy and Jack Hannent lived.
Not looking what I was doing, and probably taking imaginary pot shots at something in the sites of my pretend rifle. Meticulously thrust the stick in the front wheel, resulting in being

catapulted over the handle bars, landing on my Knee, causing a large wound. We were near to Hannents luckily Mrs Hannent was at home and took me to the Doctor at Melton constable. On the rear of her cycle. My bottom painfully wedged into the child carrier, affixed to the rear, it at least took my mind off the pain of my Injury . Four stitches in the wound, and Doctor declared I must rest the Knee.

Eleven years old in a few weeks and would have to go to the Secondary Modern School at Melton Constable, though it was still in Briston. At least I am deferred from that torture for a while anyway, I was able to burst at least one stitch climbing the plumb tree.

We had dens made of bracken and broom on the pony meadow , sometimes the old lady came over to see if we were annoying Jack the pony. A very tall Fir tree stood at the far side, we climbed it often. One time we had an idea to make a crow's nest at the top, the lid off the copper, a saw and some nails were taken over the meadow. The tree climbed, the top cut off and the lid secured at the tip. How we were able to climb over the edge of the lid and sit on top I will never know; we had a little dog called Betty. She was a fine rabbit catcher, caught some fifteen in one harvest field, before she was a year old, she was below the tree when the old lady came over. "I know where they are Betty", thinking we were hiding in the bracken, had she looked up she may have had a Fit.

I was to have started at the new School after my Birthday. However, the Knee was not ready yet, and Father took me to see the head Master, Mr Parnell, and explained the situation. It is only a matter of time now, as to how long I can use my injury to delay the obvious.
My game is up and not long after the introduction, I am going to the new School. I did not like it one little bit, I wanted to learn, but here again. My questions regarding the subjects in hand just looked upon as being an awkward pupil.

I just wanted to know in more detail than that given by the Master's. Not that I attended School in hand me downs, though I had noted the attention given to those pupil's better dressed in off the peg clothes.
My seemingly inability to grasp things, often had me deported to the garden with some other of my unlucky friends. Maybe they did not think so, out in the garden away from lessons.

But I really wanted knowledge, and the rest of my life found it the hard way. Still we had a whole new area of country side to explore.

On one of our excursions around the fields, we found an old Binder canvas, brought it home, and in the seclusion of the Broom that was some seven-foot-high on the pony meadow. Decided to make a Canoe.   With hazel nut sticks, and any spare things that Father may know nothing about. The canoe was dully built tared and sanded. Hopefully water tight.

The day came when we decided to take it to Black water, a river about two miles by road, not quite so far over the fields.

We had not gone far when spotted by the local Policeman and was questioned as to what we were doing. Not being far from the Slaughter house pit, down the stone road, we explained that we were just going to try our canoe in the pit to see if it would take in any water. We were very concerned, but he seemed to be satisfied with our explanation.

We could have been taken into custody and given three years Borstal; it was not unheard of to get punished by law for taking something that did not belong to you. Even if it were in the family, four boys I knew in two separate cases, were given three years Borstal. For no more than throwing a stone into a disused well. And the others for taking a bicycle, not with the intention of keeping it.

After a long walk we arrived at the Blackwater river. Not a big river, more of a large stream about four-foot-wide, and a foot deep in places, we had caught trout there many times. By tickling with our hands. By now the Tar that was not dry, was on our hands and clothes, the canoe did float but not well, it needed a ballast of flags and earth from the river bank, it was not very successful. Only I was able to sit in it without turning over. We abandoned the boat and our clothes and spent the day swimming in the water. With a little ingenuity one could make a Beaver dam, and soon have a nice pool to swim in, I do not remember how we got on about the Tar .

Jack Hannent found some oil drums, that had been on an old raft at the Mill. We walked with them up through the back of Craymere gardens, out onto the road, over to Holmes wood, across to Ridlands barn to Muns green, and put them out of sight at the wash pits.
Now one of the spare shed doors looked Ideal, a platform for the raft. This duly loaded onto the cart and wheeled away to the wash pits, and the oil drums.
Eventually the drums affixed to the door, not very stable, but with a rigger; could be sailed across the pond. This pond I understand, had in it some very deep parts. This does not occur to young sailors. It seems Father missed the door, and either Kenny or Dick, being younger were not invited to join our expedition. Informed of our suspected whereabouts.

In time Father arrived at the wash pits. With what he saw, was afraid to call out in case the ship founded. Mind you it had sailed the pond many times, later as we docked, his presence well assured, we and the door escorted back to Hall Street. Many of our exploits went unseen.

I am afraid I cannot say much about the school at Melton Constable, I hated the place, what I had taken in at Briston. Did I think, the extent of my real schooling? We made some things in the wood work class, I got a belting for calling a cigarette box a fag box, I made a cheese dish on the lathe, a stool, and a metal ash tray.

In music I was put to work in the garden with others of my kind, who passed some of the time, putting stinging nettles into the girl's toilets, through the door at the rear, that opened out onto the garden. I do remember something about building a garden pool. I hated physical training, a bully of a master wanted us to do cart wheels, and standing on one's head, it made me very sick. Any boy caught doing wrong, or reported for doing something wrong, by persons in the village. Were at the door to the entrance hall, caught and belted on the spot.
One lad I forget his name now, as he was being bent over for the belt, continued going forward, and dashed for safety. The hue and cry over this, one would think he had killed the master. But it was like that then .

This adventure I call. The Pilot would not Fly.
The old perambulator, that had long since lost its body to the Bully Hills, in the Snow. Its occupants descending at a rapid rate, had abandoned the safety of its confines to the Snow, as the speed of the decent, became obviously of some peril to the crew. Now watched from the snow-covered slopes, as the boat shape entered the stream at the lower reaches of the Hills. Only to fill up with water, and slowly pushed down stream by the ever-increasing volume of water building up, the dam like object impeding its course. Fighting its tormentor, the water rolled and pushed it down stream out of sight .

The Spring now forming the buds on the trees, settled down to the work of growing more willows and Hazel rods. The four wheels and chassis of the old perambulator, having given up all hopes of ever being reunited with its boat shaped body, begins to sprout Hazel rods, striped of their newly grown leaves. Two from each side, shaped and strutted to form a wing like feature to the whole contraption. As the days go by and School taking less of the valuable time, further strutting takes place, eventually a wing form, in need of covering takes shape. A supply of thick brown paper sacks, now replacing the usual sacking cloth, redly available at the corn merchants is obviously the material for the covering. After many failed attempts the wing covering is in place, glued, tacked, wetted, and dried many times, finally taut has become a rigged structure.

Now four Hazel rods protruding from within the chassis below the wing, to converge some distance to the rear, lashed together. And finally, a copy of the wing structure, though a much smaller version, duly covered stressed and mounted, on the rear section at the conversion of the four Hazel rods.

A device in the space behind the wing, truly fixed with good twine, enabling the rear wing or plane to be tilted up and down, the vertical fin of stout card board, permanently fixed forward of the tail plane.
The larger wing made to turn to a fore and aft position. As would be in the case of an Air craft Carrier. To enable the whole contraption to pass out of the garden, up the lane, onto the road, without any undue damage to the delicate structure.

Now father had arrived home one day with a, James two stroke motor cycle, all attempts to start it were to no avail. It did not take long for scheming heads. Though Father had locked away the petrol, that there was plenty of Methylated spirits, Mother used to light the primus stove, that proved to not only start the James, but a carburettor bowl full would make it round the garden, and more; before it had consumed all the fuel.

"I know they have been trying to start my Motor cycle, it is never where I leave it father exclaims".

The day duly arrived, as in true Navel tradition, with folded wing, the Machine and the James trundled out of the garden, and up the lane on to the highway. Though traffic was minimal, the side road was to be the place for the trials. Firstly, the two young one's of five to six years, exclaiming they would tell Father, found it difficult to believe that we did not reject their pleas to come with us.

James and David.

Well one of them was needed as the pilot and did not disapprove at all until on the side of the road.

The wing now lashed in prime position, rope affixed to the James carrier, the carburettor bowl topped up with methylated. Informed the chosen one to sit in the space behind the wing and hold on to the device that tilted the rear plane. All attempts of persuasion failed, and sounds of, "I will tell Father" disappearing in to the distance.
There is nothing for it but to lash the controls. The wind singing through the struts, as the structure following the James, at full throttle, and rose to a height allowed for by the length of the rope.

The last of the Methylated disappearing into the cylinder of the James, the whole structure flashes by overhead, embracing the telegraph pole conveniently appearing in the hedgerow.

Father comes in. You Boys have been trying to start my motor cycle again, I did not leave a rope around the carrier.

Next to my Grandmother's house, lived Eke. A very small house, built close to the fence, as was the way in the old days, also a definite boundary.

You can move a boundary, but not so easy a whole house

One could just squeeze by my grandmothers then, and the house. Hedges do walk to the sun, if you let them. The suckers come up and the old wood dies off behind, hence the permanent boundary by placing the wall of the house on it.

Quite a large piece of land had Mr Eke. At one end near to the pony meadow, lived Mr Anthony Eke, in a large wood hut. At the south east corner, a spring rise. This was there only water supply, it starts as a small stream and makes its way through the pony meadow on to the Donkey meadow, under the road and now part of the Bure. On through the meadow just off Growl Abby cottages.

The Bure starts at Melton Park. South of our cottage a large orchard and a bungalow. Mr and Mrs Willmott, Winey and Sid. A daughter Evelyn. Sid a guard on the railway, lost a leg in the first world war. Over from the bungalow, the gate house and Railway level crossing.

At the end of our little lane "loke". Across the road was the allotments, running to a point where the road and railway meet.
We had the first two allotments. Father had a large chicken hut and chickens; it was allotments all the way to the chapel.

There a row of cottages, in one lived Mr Strutt a blind man. Who with a basket work cart, sold small house hold items around the village, he also worked in a large black hut, near the Chapel making and repairing cane items, He also Pumped the Church Organ?
To the right of our lane another orchard, at the north west end a bungalow. I think Father said it was built for under three hundred pounds. A new house by our standards, this was; Mr Gemmell "Jack" he worked for the Coop, his wife a school teacher. Mrs Corbel of the shop lived with them. Next to them Mrs Maggie Sexton, she also had a little shop, fronting to the road and sold most things.

Mr Claxton next, a large house with a large field, chapel people had a son John, there was Edie I do not remember the others. John later was sent to Nottingham to work in the Coal mines, he was to be a Bevin boy. Tom Willmott also to the docks, for the building of the Mulberry harbour. Used in the D day landings, others were sent to the Midlands to work in the factories.

The railway, already essential service moved boys to where ever they may be used to the best advantage of the war effort. Mr Bert Barwick next house he ran the local taxi, at one time had a Trojan car, his legs were injured in the first world war, he also had a small shop over the other side of the road, sold sweets. Mr and Mrs Barwick had two children, Molly and Dick about my age. I only remember the sweets, no money to buy them with, we had no pocket money. Only when I started working, working on the railway. A wage One Pound and Four Shillings a week, then mother took one pound and I the remaining to save.
I was eleven when I first went to the cinema, three pence to go in for the Matinee. Again, after I started work then mostly once a week unless working late shift.

Mr Parker from the garage at Hindolvestone ran the cinema, with Charles Bly from the West End, and Mr Eggleton, Mr Ernie Whittered looked after the box office, He let us in free, and the best seats after we had joined the services. Mrs Rolf from the west end, she maintained law and order, no one dare misbehave, whatever the age, she would deal with them.

The lighting was off the mains, the power for the arc was from, one of two first war search light engines located at the rear. Just after they were started the main lights would go off and come on dimly at first, a shout Go on Charlie, to Mr Bly in the box, and the picture show begins.

I had yet a Year to go to School, and War had been Declared with Germany. People were putting strips of paper on their Windows; some had painted on Gelatine. All to prevent the glass from Fragmenting in case of an Air Raid. The School had started a watch on the listening Post, situated a way up the foot path opposite the old Lime Kiln workings, on the Melton road.

A small hut with a flag pole by the side, to give warning of suspected Air Raid by flying a flag up the pole. This was maned by the Observer Corps.
I had now an after-School job in the Shop at the West end, a Mr Reynolds, his son also had the Petrol pumps and cycle shop near the Church. His son in law the Garage on the Melton road, Mr Dick Eke. My wage twelve shilling a Week .

I joined the local ATC cadet force 1954 SQDN. Training sessions at the School under Mr C Futter the head Master of the Briston School. The Airfield at Foulsham was being built, some of the lads who left School the year before. We're driving lorries, carting Sand and Shingle, for three pounds a week. jolly good pay. One did not need a driving test then, just apply for a provisional Licence, cost "five shillings

I was one of the School Observers. We took turns to sit by the window in the Hall. Watching the Observer post across the field, If the flag was seen flying from the mast, a warning of imminent Air attack.

A large Bell was to be rung up and down the corridor.

With the Air training corps, we were now having some Drill, and Lectures in Aircraft Recognition, and communications, this included Morse Code that always

interested me, later to become one of my many interest's. Also, I had been supplied with a Uniform. Enabling one to get on to the Air field at Foulsham.

I left School in 1941, changed my job for one with a Baker, long hours, One Pound and three pence a week. Had to be there for first Dough, help make the second batch of Dough, do the local round with a bicycle.   Two large Baskets on the front and rear.

The alternate week, I start at eight, help with the long round, a round that sometimes lasted until Seven in the evening, then come back to the Bake house and help with late dough, that was to be the mornings first batch. The Dough was made in a hand cranking machine, this took about twenty minutes, the fire for the oven was lit very early, by Mr Garrod the owner, the fire was in part of the oven, and burnt until the oven had reached the required heat for Baking. The whole oven then swept out, with a long pool with a damp sack on the end of it. The oven would bake then all day. On Saturday, and at Christmas time, some of the local people, came to have their roasts cooked .

I soon found another job for a short time, with a firm of timber Merchants "Longhurst's". Cutting down timber for the Coal pits. One pound ten shillings a week, hooking the chains onto the timber for the machine to pull out of the wood. Often the wood came forward unsuspecting, bruising one's legs.

They were taking on Cleaners at the Railway works at Melton. I applied for a post.

In the meantime, Father had dug a large hole on the pony meadow, and started making an Air raid shelter, Railway sleepers inside and all covered with soil.

Father was an Air raid warden. One night he and I had to go down to Mr Futters house, another Warden, and later, looking for some German parachutist. Father armed with a four ten shot gun, I an Air rifle, what we hoped to achieve, who knows, they had been reported at dusk. They turned out to be some low flying Swans.

Grandmother would come up to our house if an Air raid was suspected, "no one was to make a sound" she said, "they had phones lowered down to listen for sounds".
I do believe During the Airship raids, during the first War; they did just that. The shelter was finished, it was decided much later after it had been built to use it.

An Air Raid was in progress over Norwich, so we all filed over to the pony meadow. Father was the first down, the splashing and cursing said only one thing, we would not be using the shelter tonight, in fact we never used it at all, a lot of water had seeped in since it was first built.

There must have been many German Aircraft over Briston. There was only one that caused any damage, it came up the Yarmouth Line, firing its guns over the Gate house, and the back of our gardens.
Mother said at the time she was feeding the Rabbits, we had in a hutch. It flew up the line to Melton firing its guns in the direction of the signal department, and dropped some Bombs near the main water tanks, and in Mr Jone's field. It damaged the tanks slightly; the marks remain today.

Also Killed Mr English, it was early on a Sunday morning. He had been up to the tanks to take a reading of the water level, a daily task of the LOCO department.

I at the time, and some other lads were on our way to Blakeney to get cockles, something we liked to do when we had the time. A man from Blakeney who came into the village with shell fish, had invited us to go whenever we wanted. Mr Thompson, he had a nick name, "Pintail" he lived half way up the hill from the Quay. A kindly couple gave us jam sandwiches before we returned home.

We were on the road to Sharrington and heard a commotion in the direction we were going. Guns firing into the air and on the ground, and much shouting and whistle blowing. I can't remember seeing the Aircraft, but lots of smoke in that direction. We were given the story when we arrived back home.

The search light Battery at Sharrington, had engaged the Aircraft as it fired upon them, causing it to come down further toward the Sea.

My Uncle a special Constable said, "when they located the plane one of the crew who was Dead, and had been taken out of the Aircraft, and placed by the hedge". The rest had taken with them a Rubber Dingy, and were heading towards the coast, they believed after a time that they were lost, and gave themselves up to some local people.

About the same time a Mosquito crashed on the field near to Mr Philips house.
I was looking for rabbits on my Uncle Fred's field at the time, and went over to help, at the same time the girls from Philips house were coming from the other way, they fetched water and towels, the second member of the crew had his legs badly injured.

Having helped to move them away from the Aircraft that was smelling of fuel, not feeling very well, I left and returned home. Shortly after a Policeman called, He wanted to see my gun licence, I had one. He left saying. "You can choose your friends but not your relatives". I was not quite sure what he had in mind until, Mother explained later. The Informant another Uncle, who did not like me shooting near to his place.

I was accepted as a cleaner at the Railway works. But first I must go to Norwich for a Medical, by the Railway appointed Doctor. I started the same day as Ivan Willard he lived at Melton .

Working in Essential Service's, one was exempt from call up, though not quite old enough any way, I was requested to join the Home Guard.

Now I had two Uniforms and a Gun, an Enfield 300 American rifle but no Ammunition. I was number two rifle man to a Machine gunner.

Hats Willimott was number one. We paraded by Jack Carters farm, he had been made the Officer, also his son. His son John also commanded the Army Cadet's in the Village.

Near to the road was a little hut, for night patrols, with holes in the roof, Grandad had banged down a Sten gun on the table, automatically it fired into the roof. The roll call was taken there, and the roster for night patrols. My other half was Hats, we cycled the given route, it was supposed to take two hours to complete the patrol, we made it last for half an hour.
By that time, we had arrived at the Search light Camp on the Norwich road, there we were treated to a brew up. Sometimes I was so tired, Hats would say to me, "Slip off home you will not be missed.

On one exercise the Army were to hold the wood at Stody. The Home Guard to route them out, someone fired a live round through the trees, they all came out in a hurry. I was working shifts much of the time so missed lots of the action.

Father had an Austin Seven, of 1927 vintage. Often, we would take it out, this particular occasion we had been to Binham. Brother Kenny and Bob Cushion in the rear, being near to Christmas we had the four ten shot gun in the car. Approaching Pigs Grave there was a Cock Pheasant sitting on one of the fence posts of the Railway Line. It was duly shot and put in the rear, only to recover as we drove down Melton street.
It recovered and decided to take off again. Causing unscheduled variations to our passage through Melton Constable.
I had to add this episode as having only this week been reminded about it by Bob himself

The War apart from the obvious, made little difference to the way the country folk lived, they had always had to struggle to make ends meet. Most people had a garden or allotment, and provided much for themselves, and now even more so. Father had a pig to fatten, always chickens and rabbit's in huts. Our job was to gather hog weed from the hedgerow to feed them with, we gathered Acorns in season, they could be sold for pig food, about a shilling a bushel. Hazel nuts from the hedgerow, and other seasonal fruit, bottled and stored. We gathered chestnuts and even Beach mast, though I did find the Beach mast did dry ones mouth a little, our exploits with a fishing line.
A Hazel rod with the string wound around the top. No reel then, a bent pin. For the fortunate a number fourteen hook.

We Were now favoured, for our exploits instead of being frowned upon. A large Roach from the Sand pit's or an Eel from the Beck, all helped to fill a small hole as Mother would say.

Wood gathered for the fire from the hedgerow, and a swede from the Farmers Field a blessing. Mother found a way to cook up Sugar beet, and extract the sweetness, it served its purpose, though I did not favour it, I preferred a spoonful of jam in my tea, rather than no sweetener at all. The Eggs when in good supply were stored in a large earthen wear pot, in Isinglass, they would keep for a very long time.

I remember waiting in hiding ages, for one Farmer to go away, so we were able to release a whole cage of Sparrows and Blackbirds. There must have been Hundreds trapped in his Stack yard. I am to believe they were for the pot. But this is something that had been practised in the olden days.

Father always grew enough potatoes, to see us through to next year's crop. He made a hole in the garden, locally called a hod, the potatoes covered with straw, and then earthed up all over, a tuft of straw coming out at the top to vent the hod. They kept very well that way, Chestnuts would keep that way also.

All bread was whole meal, a little white flour available if you knew the local Baker well enough, this was for the little luxuries like Current buns.
One could get Black-market Sweets, brought up from London, in exchange for white flour. I personally think people, in general; were much healthier with the Ration's provided during the War, than today's Diet.
We had our problems, yet some may have come at any time. I remember an outbreak of Scabies, a mite that got below the skin. We all had to be bathed in a very hot Bath, and scrubbed with a very rough brush, and Methylated Spirits, this was done in front of the fire in the tin Bath, I remember it well.

The War brought out the best in people I am sure, queuing for things was taken in good heart obvious everyone was in this War together. I have not seen the like of Comradeship since. and doubt will ever again.

The letter from the Loco department arrives I am to report for duty the following Monday. Mother had found some overalls that Father had grown out of, those would have to do for a time. There was a code of dress, the work would at times be very dirty.

A Bib brace overall and Jacket, later would be supplied. On gaining qualifications to become a past cleaner, a black Jacket and cap, an Overcoat later. That was changed every two years.

The Monday morning, having put my cycle in the place reserved for Loco staff, I found my way to the signing on office in the Loco. Not a very large place, it was part of the stores, and another small office, the notice on the door said Night Foremen.
A large sloping table behind the window that ran the length of the signing on, contained the Book where the Engine crews signed on and off duty, the walls hung with notices relevant to all Loco staff.

In the partition between the office and the stores a hatch way, it was through here cleaners may obtain the work ticket from the store man, also other small stores needed.

I had company. Ivan Willard was also starting as a cleaner today.
A Cleaner is the first rung of the ladder to Engine Driver. A cleaner having served his time, studied his trade and satisfied the examiner on the day of his test. Becomes a past cleaner and

now able to take Firing turns on the Footplate with either a Driver or past Fireman, or any other duties that entail's working with steam.

Having obtained the number of firing turns required. He will become qualified and hold the position, paid as a Fireman, though having to return to the shed if no firing turn is available. Later having completed the required number of Firing turns, can now qualified as a Driver.

Each Depot has an allocation of Set's. (Crew's).
In the days just before the War. It was a matter of waiting for someone to Die, or move to another Depot, where your seniority date. (The day you started with the company) fits in.

At this moment in time all the Engine Tenders, proudly display. The logo of the Company we are now working for. The London and North Eastern Railway. L.N.E.R. When possible we found delight in getting those bright and sparkling, also the Engine number on the side of the Cab. The paint work cleaned and oiled, working our own pattern into the oil. Some I for instance, with a nice clean folded cloth, worked into the glaze. The Prince of Wales Feathers. A pattern of, one central Ostrich Feather, with one either side, with Plumes opposing. If I say so myself, it looked very Hansom. As cleaners on the Railway working in the Loco, we were supposed to clean the Engines, and learn our trade as firemen.
There was not much time for Cleaning, in the cleaning gang one would be picked out in seniority the date of starting with the company.

Before it had been, the Midland and Great Northern Joint, M.&.G.N. Either for clearing up ashes or coaling, Helping the fitters, or other little jobs that came up. Ashes was fine, the work hard but one could work through the Dinner break, and leave off an hour early, the ash pits had to have the ashes from the fires and ash pans thrown out of the pits, and then up into a wagon. Wet ashes can be very heavy, there were small heaps about the Loco to be gathered up and general cleaning up. I think we got a few more pence as well.

Loading Coal or unloading Coal, to enable the wagon's to be returned. Many wagons having been destroyed in the Bombings about the Country.

The wagon repair shop was now started up in the old Carriage building shops, to keep the wagons on the road. The Coal was dumped on any spare ground by the old wagon sidings. Large lumps to make a wall the smaller Coal at the back. Damaged waggons then taken to the waggon shops for repair.

The first time we were sent unloading Coal, the whole gang went. Most of the time was spent playing Put and Take for pennies, in the carriage sidings. Until the Loco foreman came to see how we were getting on, very little had been done.

He was not amused, and said "you will all come in tomorrow, and not go home until you have unloaded fifteen tons of Coal and given Mr Grint (Storeman) the wagon ticket". We were in at four AM, and had unloaded the Coal, and washing up by the time the Foreman came on duty. Washing up was in the large static water tanks, now in place about the depot in case of fire, we found that the Russian tallow in the wagon Axle boxes made a fine soap. And plenty of that was needed. Coal heaving was a very dirty job.

The foreman was again not amused, he had not heard of Incentive.
After that we always unloaded Coal, on peace work. though It was put up to twenty Tons for a shift of one man. Or Boy I should say.

Other Coaling jobs were. The Coal Stage. Loading the little half ton trucks and pushing them over to the Coal Crane, to be lifted up to the tender of the Engine. This plant was operated by four men. Two to a shift, eight to four and Four till twelve, or when the last Engine was Coaled. We helped in busy times or had to relive one of the Coal men.

Sometimes the Crane broke down. It was quite a task then to Coal by hand, wagons were put as near to the tender as possible. Making use of converging sets of points, the Coal picked off the top by hand. When one had picked to the bottom of the truck, it was a case of shovelling up onto the tender, sometimes this was too much for young Bone's, and a platform made up with a steel sheet, the Coal shovelled up onto the sheet of steel. Then climbing up and shovel from there. There was no light at night only the flare of a paraffin torch. That choked one with its smoke.

This brief illustration of Coaling Engines at Melton can never show the very hard work and conditions the lads had to endure Coaling.
Even with the use of the crane, it was a very heart-breaking job. Yet we completed the shift and came back for some more.
At the end of the Coal stage was a large Area. During the summer when the Coal was in plentiful supply, this Area was dumped with Coal from wagons. During a shortage, it had to be wheeled back onto the Coal stage. Not only to the stage but up on to it, up planks of timber. and usually it was raining or snowing being winter time. The base of the dump, Clay now wet and slippery.
More than often just as one had just filled all twelve of the tubs, an Engine would stop for Coaling. That cup of tea and a sit down in the Coal men's mess room, had to be given a miss. They certainly made, Old Bones of young ones.

After a time, one having learned the essentials of lighting up Engines, and maintaining steam. Knocking up was another job. The shift started on a Sunday night. Twelve one AM, I left home on my cycle about Eleven, so as not to disturb the rest of the family later on.

There were jobs to be done in the Loco, when the jobs were done time was your own.

The Approach to the works on a Sunday night, was to say A little frightening to a young lad. The Street of Melton silent, only the gas lamps fluttering away at the top of their standards. Later these though shaded were turned off, just in case Aircraft flying low could see them. Then it was knowing your way or mind your head.

Looking down over the Loco, from the Hindolveston road. The Turntable dimly lit from the odd Gas Jet spluttering away on the shed wall. To the left, Lord Hastings waiting room, and the Station platform, Beyond the table, the Engine men mess room, and stores, in the distance the Canopy of the Coal Stage, with the Water tanks rising above and to the right. The running shed was to the right of the Table with the Fitters workshop at the end. The Boiler smith and washer out crew, also had a hide away there.

To the right of the running shed. The Chair legs for lifting Engines for bearing work in the machine shop. The sand hole was this side also, the sand was dried here, and sieved to make it fine for running through the pipes from the Engine sand boxes, on to the line, to prevent the wheels from slipping. We baked potatoes in the wet sand.
Also, if making a lighter from a cannon shell, one could melt out the lead from the bullet. I put one in once and it was a tracer shell, fortunately I had closed the sand hole door. The explosion was contained, the shells were easily found in the fields near the Airfield.

One lad I knew, without taking the bullet out of the shell, put one in a vice and hit the firing cap with a nail, the result was a loud bang some badly scratched knuckles. The bullet stayed in the vice; the case took off vertical never to be seen again.

On a clear night, one could see all over the Loco from up on the road. On a dark night, rather a frightening place, before it was brought back again to life. With the glow from the fires and the hissing of steam the smell of hot oil, the comparison could not be different. Remember we were but lads of some five teen years, more than often working alone doing responsible work.

The night foreman arrives. Mr Gilbert Smith (Gunboat) I do not know where he got that name from. He had been doing that job for many years, never saw light of day some say. He unlocks the stores and night foreman office, and we book on. The signing on was part of the stores.

The little sliding door between the stores and the signing on was called the Wika. The wika was where cleaners obtained the materials from the store man for cleaning Engines, a large tin full of paraffin and cloths. There were New ones, seconds and washed. New ones were for handling hot steam keys and levers.

The task of the knocker up on a Sunday night. Monday morning was a little different to the rest of the week, the mess room to be cleaned out, the day time Loco foreman's office to be cleaned out and the fire remade, had it been used.
The night foreman gives the list of Engines to be made ready for Monday morning, and the order of lighting up. The firelighter house was by the day foreman's office. Bundles of shavings bounded by four sticks and soaked in some chemical, that burned one's eyes as the door to the house was opened, two to each Engine. Each boiler checked to see if it had enough water in for lighting up. There were two-gauge glasses on each boiler, lit by a small paraffin lamp hung behind the gauge, each Engine firebox given a good quantity of coal, leaving a space just under the door for the fire lighters to be placed when lighting up, about two hundred weight. All prepared and back to the office.

Also, the boiler over the sheet factory, and the boiler over the signal department had to be got ready, it was a long walk over to the signal department and a little frightening. It was over there that the man was machine gunned and killed by the German Aircraft.
The Factory boiler was no better. One was continuously looking around at the shadows.

The foreman goes over the list of Engine men to be called early. Knocking up was just to see if the appointed crew were available for duty.

The Engines were lit up according to the time they would have to be ready for the crews, as they came on duty. Allowing time for the fire to get going and raise steam enough, to get the blowers going if needed, and the Injectors working to top up the boilers.

In between times, the crews in order as given by the foreman, were visited at their homes. A knock at the door would get a response. Usually, right Ho.

As I got use to the job, I would stay at the Gas works, sitting by the retorts in the warm. There was always a man on duty there, not only was the Gas used at the works. It supplied the whole of Melton Constable, I would only walk all the way back to the Loco, to light the next Engine on the list, or go around those that were making steam, and would be needing attention.
The sheet factory and Signal department boiler were the last to be lit up. The signal department boiler was actually for pumping the water, from the well to the main tanks. The sheet factory boiler for the radiators in the factory when it was cold. They not only repaired the sheets there but made new ones.
Not due off until eight but having arrived early, I could get away by seven. As the Engines would be looked after by the crews or shed steam raisers who came on at eight.

Often a cleaner gets this job, and usually the sand hopper to look after, and plenty of time to sit up in an Engine cab and read the rule book. One had to be learning all the time, asking the old hands things that were not clear to one, learning the rules off by heart. The Railway runs by the rule book when it suits them, all the things one may encounter on main line, this is difficult to grasp before ever going on the main line.

As cleaners we often rode the footplate through to Holt and Corpusty On the School trains, just a short trip but one way of getting the experience.

Not that the rule book allowed that sort of thing. The past cleaner's examination was the first real examination, it gave one the chance to actually take a firing job, on the pilot in the yard, or go main line. And the completion of the required number of firing turns, gave one the title of Fireman. But this did not ensure a firing job full time, there had to be a vacancy in the depot, of the same seniority date as one's own.

The date you started on the Railway. This is why many passed cleaners moved away to get promotion in the grade, to where there was a shortage of Engine crews.

The wage was for a fireman £4/13/and sixpence, for a 48-hour week. As a cleaner my weekly wage was. £1/4 shillings. Some days the Cleaning gang could talk of nothing but the past cleaner Test. Sometimes the whole gang was on shed, with only cleaning to do, certain ring leaders would think up some practical joke on some unsuspecting person.

One time the toilets had to be white washed, two of the seniors appointed for the job, and duly arrived on site, armed with white wash and long brushes, one of the toilets were occupied, "Grandad" he would not come out, so he was white washed along with the rest of the toilet.

He was also fair game when the food boxes were left in the mess room, the box quite a large trunk, the standard box for Railway men to carry their food, and other things one may need. The box was emptied a nail drove through the bottom into the table top and the food replaced, sometimes after the food was eaten you may find the box filled with Coal.

A driver from Wells used to bring shell fish at times, and the place was like a shell fish bar, shell fish roasting on the fire, mussels were a favourite of a pall of mine. Many times we had been together to Norwich, to try to volunteer for the Royal Navy without success, he had placed them on the fire grate to cook, they must have not been done properly, as within a few days he was very Ill, and off work for months, and much later refused entry into the Navy, due to medical grounds.

Sometimes we were caught in the mess room by the foreman, the mass exit from the little side window must to have been seen, to be believed.

Another time the early gang were sitting in Engine cabs, out of the way, before the day foreman came on duty. Many Solders were standing by the edge of the platform waiting for the Leicester to run in from Yarmouth, they had been throwing Thunder Flashes over into the Loco. Two of the gang went up to the Coal stage and over to the platform, to work down below them without being seen, and with a whole tin of Detonators, fixed the lot on the line just below the soldiers' feet. In come the train, twelve loud bangs, on go the brakes and the train stops short.

The night foreman being in on the act, shouted out. "He has stopped the so and so". This was going to cause some real trouble for someone.

In turn we paraded into the day foreman office, he was going to sack the lot, if we did not say who put the detonators down. No one would give the others away, so between the Station Master and the Foreman they agreed to drop it, no more was heard about it.
It was not the Detonators they were concerned about but the train stopping in section. Certain procedure had to be taken to move the train forward those few yards.

On one of our Coal unloading ventures, it was decided to climb into the old M&GN carriage store, in a whole row of little boxes were the Chamber pots, for the sleeper cars. Who is on knocking up next week? Well next week on the Monday morning, Melton folks who cared to look up to the gas lamps, saw an array of Chamber pots swinging from the lamp post. I wonder who drew the short straw.

It was like a holiday over the week end, the Education cars had been placed in the Loco, up on the siding near to the foreman office. They would remain there until those who had need of the Instruction had been through them. There were sectioned Injectors, so one could see the inside workings.
And many other interesting things, wicks all made up, something only seen in the oil boxes. They were to feed the oil in a controlled way from the box to the bearings. It was not long before some were told off for scrounging off cleaning duties.

On a very hot day a few would go missing, only to be found up at Melton Lake, Swimming. All in all, I do not think any serious crime had been committed.   After all every cleaners ambition was, to get that examination over, and onto the next stage.

At Melton the Inspector arrived. It was thought that some of us were ready for the Past Cleaners Test. In anticipation the gang looked very busy at their task in hand. No one wanted to be left out this time, in due time the foreman came down the shed and told one of the gang to report to the office, it seemed ages before the lad returned to send the next one in, my turn eventually came.

The night Foreman's office was being used by the Inspecting officer, who was a very pleasant man. Questions asked on the rule book, what would you do if the train stopped in section, how would you prepare the engine for the road, and lots of the things we had been learning out of the rule book.

I thought I made a mess of the answer to the signal boards, the shape of a distant board and so on, one had to remember that, at times they would be covered in snow. Only the shape would show which board it was.

I returned to the shed, this part was over, would I be called for the practical test. This Involved working as the fireman on main line.

The day arrived. I was to report to the platform where the train for Norwich was waiting to leave.   The fireman was getting into the carriage, he was to ride on the cushions.
The driver, I have long forgotten. The Inspector said, "Forget I am here". I made out I knew what I was doing, looked into the fire, that had already been looked after for me, opened the taps on the water gauges testing to see that they gave a correct reading, and took my place, Fireman's side, keeping a sharp look out for the right away signal from the Guard.

The whistle and the green flag, and a right of way mate to the driver. The train starts to move away past the East Box, and over to the starter signal for the Norwich road. I Look over to the driver, "Right away mate", the advanced starter off, keeping a sharp look out, making sure the Inspector see me. Put the Injector on as we get under way, putting some water into the boiler, keeping a sharp look out for any gate boards, or whistle boards.

The gates where the land owners may cross the line over the fields.

The Hindolveston distant, and home board in sight and off, I tell the driver. He has seen them anyway, we run into the Station, the first section completed.
We pull away for Guestwick. It was just along here that a passenger train came off the rails about five years previous.

I remember going to see it. Some bright lad had written on the side of the train. All change for Guestwick.

I looked at the shovel, not quite sure if I should fire the box. A nod from the driver and my attempts were, that most of the coal ended up all over the cab, yet some where it needed to

be. With one leg fixed behind the handbrake, the other wedged by the seat, it was still quite a skill to stay in one place, while one half of the cab rolled one way, and the tender the other.
I must have made the right Impression. As when the train stopped at Guestwick, the Inspector got off and into the coaches, leaving me to the rest of the journey with only the driver.

The WAR must have been in need of railway men. The Engine was one of the M&GN passenger types A (W Class), may have been a Johnson, the big driving wheels rolling violently from side to side, something one would get used to. The other fine Engine's at Melton were the Great Eastern Claud Hamilton, A full sided cab giving much more protection than the W. Not that any gave much protection running tender first, from Yarmouth to Melton in the Snow, Rain, and Hail. I am sure would dampen the enthusiasm of the hobby railway men to day. However, I must not be unkind, without the Enthusiasm of this band of devoted Boy's and Girl's. Something that Arouses our Memories. Would have been lost forever.

At last, I am a Past Cleaner, have shovel will travel.

As a past cleaner, one could now take part in a split. A split was when, a driver was booked on duty with a past fireman, the past fireman being qualified to drive, a past fireman had also to know the road, for the journey he was about to take. He could sign as knowing the road, any roads he was, or had become unfamiliar with, he may ask to ride over as a passenger, to familiarise himself again.

This also applied to a driver. The driver in charge of the train. Had to know all the signals and lights, sets of points, and where they went, and anything applying to the route.

This would be the type of crew on the Pilot, in the shunting yard, also on the shed moving, and putting away Engines, and turning Engines on the Turntable. All the shed duties that required a qualified driver, should a special train be called for.
Or a crew calling for relief, having been on duty long hours and not completed their journey. A split was then called for.
A past cleaner in seniority, from off the shed or from other Loco duties, he may have been doing. With another past cleaner, would split with the crew off the pilot or shed, or any other like crew that happen to be around at the time, one cleaner to go with the driver, and one with the past fireman. Now we have two crews, one for the pilot or shed, and one to take on the extra work that has come along.

It worked in different ways but basically the same. If one was working on the Coal stage at the time of a split, it was a God send, this was the job no cleaner wanted. One week I was split every night, just as I was coming on for, four o'clock Coal stage. Either for the sugar beet trains, or the Ammunition trains going to Yarmouth.

I remember the first Yarmouth. It was a wet dark night, crossing the boards to the Engine waiting for relief, the light from the fire in the ash pan, was lighting up the wet boards and rails, the spokes of the wheels encircled by steam from the Injector overflow pipe, the noise of Coal being put into the firebox. The fireman who was about to be relived did not mind how much work he done now; in a few minutes he would be on the cushions going back to his own Loco. The line to Corpusty was double track no need here for the key, known as the tablet. A device for single line working. The tablet was taken by each train through each single line section, at each signal box, a double track to enable trains to pass.

The tablet taken by the signal man, placed in the device in the signal box, allowing another train into that section. This way it was impossible to have more than one train in a section at one time. To pass the tablet by hand was slow.
A Melton man had invented, so I believe the tablet catcher. Before that, the fireman had adapted a way of hanging on to the uprights with his legs, holding the tablet in its pouch, a large ring handle protruding from the pouch, in such a way that the signal man and fireman were able to exchange tablets on the move.

The tablet catcher that had been devised, was affixed to the Tender just behind the hand brake coulomb, it could be moved in and out, making it much easier to put the tablet into the device. Still a few were dropped, causing delays and a lot of paper work, the signal man had the same device and the exchange was made at speed.

I should mention here an accident that happened to Sam Adams. A passed fireman at the time. They were running into Melton. It was said, that he was in the act of putting the tablet into the catcher, had left it rather late and the signal man's catcher struck Sam at about the elbow, the jaws of the Catcher were pointed and split his fore arm.

The story goes. The local Doctor was called to the platform, Sam needed Hospital treatment. The driver Mr Walpole (Punch), Hooked the Engine on to one coach, while the right of way was being arranged by the powers that be. When clear took off without a fireman to Norwich. It is said, "punch was seen going through Hindolveston", shovelling like hell in his shirt sleeves. The whole journey took twenty minutes from start to stop.

Sometimes weeks go by, and no chance of a split, calling up was now the domain of the new comer's, the occasional day with the fitters, mostly if they had a Chair legs, lift for metal work to a big end. The job of cranking the winch, lifting the Engine, was ours, it took quite a long time to lift three inches. Two men to each handle, four men (Boys).
The Coal men at the time were two to a shift. Mr Becket, and Mr Williamson, one shift, and Mr Billy Adams my Uncle, and his mate Mr Joe Horne, the other shift.

They did not always see eye to eye. Billy would get angry, and let off a few choice words, Joe on the other hand tried to smooth things over, only to make them worse. Joe was a devoted Salvationist, a man who after the tubs were full on the Coal stage, enjoyed nothing more than sitting in the Coal men's mess room under
the water tanks. The pumping Engine long having been removed and telling tales of his youth. He told me of the days he was a sinner, smoked one ounce of tobacco a day, and liked a drink, he told me tales about the horsemen of his youth.

One of his first jobs, had been boy to a gang of men doing a harvest. He told of how they all slept up in the loft of the stables, those who had far to go home.

A large pot over a fire in a grate, at one end of the stables. Filled with water and milk, and any other vegetables available. Meat sometimes, that was rabbit, or any other game that may fall prey during the days work, his job was to keep the place clean, and the pot topped up. This was the evening meal, at the end of the day's work that started at first light. And before for those men who had horses to see to.

In the morning, the pot had cooled overnight, and the contents solid, this now cut out, a piece taken by each workman with him for the mid-day meal, he never said what wage he received.

He told me a tail of a man who was in a public house, who when a horse man had stopped outside for a rest, did ask the Horse man for a drink, he had spent all his money, the Horse man refused.

On leaving the public house, his horses would not move, however he tried. Not until he went back and bought the old man a drink, was he able to go on his way, he told me how to get the powers of the Devil. With a walking Toad, many of his tales at the moment I have forgotten, and better they stay that way.

We still made occasional trips to a local Air field for flights. One evening at the A.T.C. meeting, we were told to report to the Air field on Sunday, as in view of the annual camp at Water Beach.
We were to be giving some Flying experience, it was thought better to see how one got on in the air.

The day arrived and we all lined up to get into the aircraft. A Domini Nr ZY260, all seats were full, and all told not to move about the aircraft.

After take-off, some fools found it quite fun to do just the opposite, if it had not been for the seriousness of the situation, it could have been quite funny.

In due course we had the week camp at Water Beach air field. We were shown all the things that we might encounter, in the RAF eventually. I do believe I was the only one to do so out of the whole ATC flight. The highlight of the week was a trip in a Stirling MK 1. TB9091S. F/LT Williamson Pilot. In turns we were taken up into the Cockpit and allowed to take the controls.

Now with the Home Guard we had a trip out to Trimingham, taken by lorry and dumped in a farm yard. Sorted into our respective groups, given five rounds of live ammunition, and told to march off. At the edge of a field we stopped, in front a large clump of trees at the edge of the cliff, to the right a machine gun firing over the land we were about to cross. "When the firing stops, charge the trees firing from the hip". The Voice said.
It was all ok until my rifle got entangled in hats webbing making a hole in his pouch. I suppose it could have been worse.

During another trip to Foulsham Air field, they had a JU88, going around the airfields giving the aircrews an insight into its controls, should they need to borrow one to get home with.

I often thought, what would the guns on our coast think of that. It was very narrow inside, I was able to crawl all over it, had I been a German and could drive it, that would have been very tempting.
I was often surprised at the ease, one was able to get into the air, just ask at the B flight office "anything going up," and most times, directed to one of the crew huts. To ask the crew, who usually remarked. "Find a parachute and its ok".
That was no bother, they did say you could not get out of a Michel with a parachute anyway.

Oulton air field was one of the places we went for circuits and bumps. "Take-off and landing practice". Usually sitting in the bomb Aiming position, up in the nose. Sometimes just an Air test or Gunnery practice at Sea, that was much longer trip.

One of the lads who had borrowed a parachute, and found it was the property of one. "Bill Edridge". well known as a Cricketer. Foulsham also, stored the Horsa Glider, and trained Army personnel to fly them in preparation for the forthcoming Arnhem landings.

The bug bites, and another trip to Norwich to Volunteer, sent home again. Spent the rest of the day in Backs public house, returning home by the last passenger train from Norwich.

What a sight, it had rained. The best Sunday Suite, the Trilby hat, white silk Scarf, soaked to the skin and very much worse for wear.
And we had been into Jerome to have our photographs taken. Those I am sure were lost by the way.

On nights again. lighting up, I had just swopped with Aubrey Dent one of the fitters, something for a Trombone, I fancied myself as a musician. I Put it away in the mess room and started with my duties. It was not long before the Air raid purple was sounded or rather called out, an advanced warning. All lights out, except those needed to work with, later Air raid Red, all lights out, stop work. After sitting a while, I decided to liven things up. I got out the Trombone, stood in the middle of the turntable, rendering my version of Colonel Bogy, at two o'clock in the morning. Gilbert, the night foreman was in fits of laughter he could hardly stand.
Knocking up during the rest of the week was a little different from the Sunday night turn. Booking on at Ten O'clock, the whole Loco would still be alive, and would have to remain so. On a fine night the view on arrival at the road overlooking the Loco was a different scene from the Sunday night.

Over Lord Hastings waiting room, the canopy of the platform, lit by a dull glow from the lamps that had to be left on, the sound of the shunter working over in the goods yard near to the cattle pens, and goods office, a yellow ring of light from the shunter's hand lamp, that suddenly turns to Red, as he shunts off a waggon. The Engine on the turntable, wisps of steam eerily disturbed by the figure, that climbs down from the Cab of the Engine, about to be turned and disposed of, before being put on the shed.

The Jib of the Coal crane swings showing its light as it tilts. It is remarkable how Loco Departments avoided being bombed during the War. One has to have light to work.

The warning system seem to have worked out fairly well.
The heavy thudding, as large lumps of Coal are dropped into an empty tub, they are still busy on the Coal stage. A crew coming out of the mess room just going off duty, momentarily illuminated by the light from the mess room.
Another Engine being disposed of on shed. A fierce glow of fire embers and slack, being removed from the fire box, and passed through the uprights, and dropped on to the ground in a flurry of sparks.

At the end of a journey the slag having been formed on the bars in the box, has to be removed to make the fire clean for the next journey, all the good embers are put to one side, while the slag on the bars is broken up with a long handled   tool,. Called a Pricker and lifted out with the slack shovel, and dumped to the ground, for the ash men to clear up. The fire now made up to maintain steam and water in the boiler over night, or until the Engine is required again.

First to book on and enquire of any special duties one may have been left to do, then to the routine of going around the Engines in steam making sure that the fire did not get to low or the water in the boilers, this was achieved by the use of the injector on the Engine. A device that used the pressure of the steam in the boiler to force water into the boiler.

At first this may seem impossible, the pressure being equal, yet the Injector a cleaver device using the fact that, water is relatively solid to the steam is able to using the equal pressure to force water into steam. Therefore, filling the boiler with its own pressure.

The offices to be cleaned out, and sometimes two sets of tubes to be swept out.

The boiler has a large number of tubes running from the fire box to the smoke box, about two inches across, they convey the smoke and ash through the boiler to the smoke box, also in the smoke box, the blast pipe, above the blast pipe, the funnel Petticoat. The shape of which causes a vacuum in the smoke box, as the blast of exhaust steam strikes it, adding to the force of air passing through the fire box, making the fire burn very hot.

The tubes have to be kept clean, a terrible job at the best of times. In the rain one's hands get very sore from the long-handled tool one has to slide to and fro sweeping the tubes. It has a large eye at one end, by passing a number of tows through the eye a mop is made, this passed through the tubes cleaning them. Wind blowing soot on to wet flesh burns the skin, and this was supposed to be a Boys job, only the light from a paraffin torch to see what one was doing. I am surprised that not more boys fell into the pits below. The torch, it was much like an oil can with a wide spout, tow was threaded down the spout into the body of the torch, then filled with paraffin and lit, the more wick out of the spout, the lighter, and more smoke.

Much of the tube sweeping was done by the wash out shed staff, I am pleased to say.
The calling up was as usual, but none to light up, only on occasions, going around and round maintaining steam was the norm until six o'clock came. The crews were coming on and one may wash up and go home

The beet season gave the past cleaners the chance of a few more firing turns .

Most of the small stations and halts, had a siding, wagons were available for the farmers to load the sugar beet into.
Having been brought to the station by horse and cart and loaded by hand into the wagons.
These duly collected by the shunts that were laid on by the company, or by-passing goods

picking up as they go, and brought into Melton goods yard, where the trains were made up, and all together taken to King's Lynn sugar beet Factory.

In the yard, a wagon was reserved for the beet that were left on the ground, or became dislodged during shunting, those picked up by the shunters and yard staff were put into the wagon, when full, taken to the beet factory, the proceeds then sent to the Railway Mission. A nice gesture by those concerned.

I have seen many small land owners, loading at night with oil lamps, to get the beet into the factory before it closed for the season.

If I were going past Briston gates on a firing turn I made sure to have a large lump of coal handy to push off on to our allotments. Mother would collect it with the wheel barrow, a good half hundred weight sometimes.

I am booked Cromer Beach next week. Attending Engines in steam, a lonely job but one everyone liked. Start Monday night, ride the last passenger down to Cromer, and over to the little Loco.

They had a small shed, two tank Engines and a tender Engine. The Loco Driver foreman, Mr Ted Garwood meet's you at the shed, give Instructions of what Engine he wanted Coaled. They usually wanted one Coaled, sweep the shed, and clear up any ashes, maintain in steam any Engines that were in steam, and Call him at his house, if he was on early.

There was a little mess hut about four-foot square, a large iron stove. In between times I lit the stove and later had to leave the hut it was too hot.
I had to sit outside between the times going around the Engines. I nodded off on many occasions.
The last task was to go and call Ted and catching the train back to Melton.

One can still see where Ted lived, from the new Super Market looking towards the Sea, standing by its doors you are practically standing in the Loco.

The lads are looking at the notice board often now, many vacancies are listed. I had tried for Mexborough in Yorks. later Ivan Willard and I, applied for Colwich in Nottingham. They had vacancy's in our seniority date.

In time the notice came through, Ivan and I had procured the vacancy's we applied for at Colwich.

He left a week before me. I needed a decent cycle for going to work on, as I hoped to lodge at Gedling. One of my uncles lived there. Either with them or nearby. We heard of a cycle for sale at Edgefield. Nearly new, with chain oil bath, three speed and lights. They wanted four pounds for it, quite a lot of money. Father came to some agreement, also a trouser press was thrown in as well.

In due course, I arrived by train at Nottingham Victoria Station, and cycled up to Gedling. My Aunt was at home, all enquires were fruitless, in other words they were not going to be very helpful, only to say Milly, another aunt lived down in Lambley, the next Village on the Lowdham road. A lot of time had been wasted it was getting dark when I arrived at Lambley, the house was near the Nags Head public house. Next door as a matter of fact, her husband was in the Navy , they had three girls the oldest was just over a year old and twins, but I was made very welcome. I expect she was glad of the company, and why bother looking for lodgings when a spare room was going begging.
And that is how I came to land up at Lambley, it was a very nice quiet Village, a little shop, the family I think was Radford's. Sneaths lived over in the council houses, friends of Millys. Mrs Bennet whom I repaired a sink for, she gave me a Medallion, she said "I have not a lot of money", not that I
wanted any payment. "Keep this and you will never be really short of money".

I have it still today. I think her prophecy may have been somewhere near the truth.

Milly had a garden up on the Woodborough road, in my spare time I dug and planted, can't remember what, but some pleasant times were had up there. The walks another pleasant pastime, the fields were not as at home Coveted by some land owner. It seemed, all free for one to roam the grassland, and pick the Cowslips. Something I had not seen before, though living in the country. It was in Nottingham I saw my first Magpie. They are back in Norfolk now I am pleased to say. I Visited the City but not often. The Town Hall with its two large Lions amazed me. Rock cemetery those large caves. The large park where the Goose Fair was held. The bus company was Bartons if I remember rightly. My social life did not extend to much. I have certainly been moving about for my age. Not quite sure about that, but I did have my 21St in a tent in Egypt, at Elhamra. And I have quite a way to go before that. Now I must get back to Colwick Loco.

I went down to Colwick on the Saturday afternoon. Quite a cycle ride, Wicket hill the first climb, in fact it was uphill all the way to top to Mapperley plain, and the Gedling turn off, a gentle run down to the bridge over the Railway line leading to the Gedling Tunnel, and down into Netherfield.

Just one farm house to the right about half way between the Gedling turn and the Railway bridge at the bottom, a lonely ride. Not that it bothered me, I was used to riding at night in the country.

Netherfield quite a busy little place. Colwich Loco was just a little way on down a road that was a dead end, stopping at the Railway property. A large Canteen for the staff, plenty of food if you had the money, fancy cakes and large mugs of tea all off ration. All we got at Melton was an extra quarter of tea and two pound of sugar a month, for those eating away from the Depot.

At the entrance to the sheds, were the time keeping offices, and main offices.

The Loco Superintendent was, Mr Fish. He had been at Thorpe Norwich before that. It was he who gave me a ticking off saying, "He expected more from a Melton man". I had failed to turn up at Nottingham Victoria, reliving a main line crew, the fireman had to go on with the train. This I had done with intention.

I had been yet again refused permission to join the Navy. Being on Essential service this was not permitted. He warned next time it would be the Shire Courts for "Avoiding the WAR effort".

They used to send out a form with a space for an explanation, for this kind of misdemeanour. It was common place to draw a wall with a head looking over, saying, What! no explanation, in the space.

Through the sheds to the ash pits, where in a little hut at one end, was the running foreman office. The ash pits were manned by shed staff, not Loco staff. This was their main job, cleaning out Engine fires and ash pans, at the other end of the pits, the Coal plant, there the whole wagon lifted up and tipped into the hopper of the plant. All needed to Coal an Engine was to pull a lever.

In the running foreman office, I find my name listed with, Driver Albert Lane, to be my mate for the rest of my stay at Colwich. We were roster four O'clock Stavely.

Next time I arrived at the Loco it was getting dusk, not much of an outlook starting at a new job in a strange place. It was some time before I found the allotted Engine, a Class T3 locally named Tangoes. A very large heavy three-cylinder goods Engine. Albert duly came on the Engine and introduced himself. The Engine prepared and proceeded out of the Loco and into the goods yard, to hook onto the Iron Ore train for Stavely. Albert was a jolly chap we got on well, he said he had seen Ivan, and now with me there was a need for two interpreters at Colwich. He says, "No one can tell what your swedes are talking about". Strangely, I never saw Ivan all the time I was at Colwich. We were both in the same link, the "Peterbough Link". There were thirty-two different jobs in our link, with thirty-two starting times, it was the luck of the draw to be on shed at the same time.

The Loco and yards, a maze of lines and signals. I wondered would I ever get to know where they all go to. Albert had been in this Loco all his life except the time he was driving the small Diesel Engines at the front, during the first World War. He told me tales of the German Loco men doing the same task at a hand wave distance. War a very strange thing.

The Stavely run was a hard run. First the Gedling tunnel, sometimes it was full of slime from the sulphur dropping from the roof, especially if following another train through, by the time one arrived out into the fresh air everything was covered in yellow sludge, to be washed off with the slacker hose. Eventually we run into the Iron works at Stavely an unforgettable experience. The retorts were just opening to drop the coke into the wagons below. A wall of white fire something I will never forget.

The train of Ore we had just delivered came from Nr Belvoir; it was called the Belvoir run as I remember. With that job.
One left the main line at Botsford to Barkestone. It was quite a run up with a small Engine to Denton. The fire Box needed to be full, not much chance of getting any on after getting under way, it would go straight up the tubes, and out of the funnel. If I remember rightly the Engines, we used for that run were, Retford Pacific's, the track and the gradient having no approach run up.

From the start of the Gradient. It was regulator full over, valve gear on the stop, keep the Firebox door shut, or it would suck anything loose in.

At the Ore works the fireman's job was to go over to the Keepers cottage quite a walk, to find out if there were any rabbits or game going, anything to help out the rations was helpful, not sure of the name of the place now it could have been Denton.

Some jobs were much longer than a day's work, yet not much good asking Control for relief, unless one had at least fourteen hours on. Sometimes awaiting Engine may take up to four hours and by the time one was away, it could be six hours on duty.

The Peterborough run with Coal, a one to be remembered. With a Tango hooked up to sixty wagons a clear dark night, the heavy beat of those three cylinders belching steam into the funnel petticoat, causing the fire that filled the fire box, to heave as though being lifted from below by some invisible force.

My first trip on that job I thought the fire had gone out, as we left Loco to go on to the train. Albert had looked in the box, saying we will not get far with that. I had fired up the M&GN way, a good fire
but not good enough for the Peterbough run.

Albert had spent most of the time getting out on to the train filling up the box, the size of a small room. At the beginning of the bridge over the river Trent.
The fire well and truly through showering ash up and out, falling hissing into the water, steam belching from the safety valves. Injectors singing forcing water into the boiler, a long way to go and often one gets stopped, to let more important traffic through. Being late away one lose position in the time table, hopefully relief will be waiting at Peterbough and a ride home on the cushions.

Many is the time I have fallen asleep on my cycle going down Wicket hill into Labelling one of the Peterbough runs we were riding back on the cushions a Friday. Instead of going back to Colwich, I took the train to Melton. My working clothes and my large food box was my pass, no one would know where I was going on or off duty. We had to pay our fare when off duty though reduced. Albert booked me off as usual, though I was a day short that week, The Saturday.

We also had a fast goods that changed over with the March crew at Sleaford, often they boxed up the Engine to save firing up on the move. By filling up the fire box much more than necessary, the results were that the fire had to be cleaned before we could get under way again. Their trip had been on virtually flat rails, we had now to work the gradients. To do so with a fouled-up box would have been foolhardy to say the least. Especially with the Atlantic Pacific.

We had a Mablethorpe passenger run in the link, mainly to give the Mill and Factory workers a break at the Seaside. The children with their little carts waiting at the station to earn a copper or two they were really vending for custom. The like I did not see again until I landed up in Egypt very much later.

Many of our jobs were quite nice. At one time when going through the Derby countryside, I was tempted to drop off and try to get work on one of those little Farms. We were a seven day a week job, as a young man this was not what I wanted to do for ever.
Other lads I saw, were going out just as we were starting work, there was little time for leisure. Had I have left my post following that foolhardy temptation. I would have been taken before the Courts, and there would have been the possibility of a Prison sentence. For Evading the War Effort.

On one of our shunts, I think it was Hucknall Colliery shunt, we had some time and I went up to the Bevin boys Hostel. My luck was in, John Claxton a local lad had just come off duty, and we were able to have a few words. Now that was something I would not want to do, go down those pits.

Things that stay in one's mind, Shunting the Colliery sidings took one by the backs of the Miners houses, the tin baths hanging from the walls, the white bags, of cottage cheese dripping away to make the spread to go on the bread for snap. I understood that this was used a lot down the pit, other spreads would go rancid underground.

My Uncle who lived at Gedling was top foreman there, I saw very little of them, they were Harry and Eva Hendry. They were at the VE party at Arthur's house in Bullwell. VE day took everyone by surprise.
We were running through the water troughs at Essendine, lights all over the place lots of shouting expected to go into a Bomb crater any moment, at the box the signalman shouted it's all over, it still took some time for it to sink in.

In the street just outside Arthur's house a pile of anything that would burn was lit. I remember very little after the fire was going. Fetching beer from the public house at the end of the street in a bucket, In the morning people laying everywhere. I do not think anyone went home to sleep. Arthur's front room was full of sleeping people who had to be pulled out into the street to make room to move, to get lunch made. I doubt we shall ever see such comradeship again. My call up papers arrived. Report to the Recruiting Office in Sheffield.

I hope my little story will relate in one way or other, the part very young lads played in the defence of the Country. As much if not more than their Uniformed Counterparts. Without any or very little recognition for their actions, Be it in the Coal mines, Factories or other Essential services.

I wonder what the reaction would be today, if young persons of some sixteen years of age were directed to other parts of the Country, to live and work with complete strangers.

The Blue Uniform
At last I obtain my release to join the RAF
Many who were fighting the War, whilst myself traveling the country side with my mate in a "Steam locomotive" . Pulling various goods including Petrol, Bombs, and Ammunition; from the Midlands to the Docks. I think the LNER had diversion in mind by allowing the Fireman to Attend his fire as he steamed through the country side, Illuminating the sky for many miles with no other protection than a flimsy sheet of tarpaulin lashed to the cab and down to the Tender rail. Diverting the attention of enemy Aircraft from their original target's. None spotted "Us" I am glad to say.

All those young men in their Blue Uniforms all nice and clean and out on the Town when we were just starting the nights work for all ungodly hours, try as I may to get myself one of those uniforms was always met with, You are essential to the country;" Essential Services" and stay where you are.

However in late 1945 having intentionally not turned up for duty, a main line relief for the Sheffield Express at Nottingham Victoria, the fireman now having to complete the journey on extra time; knowing this would cause a little bother, was not surprised when in my mail box in the Loco clocking on at Colwick, was the expected Brown form ,"It is requested that an explanation for your absence regarding the relief of the Fireman of the Sheffield Express. This was normal in any case of unauthorised absence. At that time a picture of a little face looking over a wall was often found in situations where one could not explain oneself, I was always a bit of an artiste and was sure my attempt would be received with some admiration. It was not and the look on the Superintendent's face assured me I may be in for a little bother.

Well he said eventually I was expecting more from a Melton Constable man " he had been the Super at Norwich Thorpe," Melton was one in his command, the War is just over or you would have been up to the Nottingham Shire Hall "The Court" for evading the War Effort, however I sympathise with you young men and you are not the only one, he became quite Human; smiling; I expect I would have been the same if I were many years younger, if you still want to go, your release will be approved.

I was back at the Recruiting office on my next day off , just nineteen years old and today would probably have still been at School, not with five 1years hard labour under my belt .

Now that Blue Uniform and nice clean work was a probability more than just a dream, little did I realize in under two years I would be sitting in a Tent in Egypt, homesick and missing the smell of "smoke oil and Steam, in as much as I started writing my story in a little red exercise book and after all those years and many little red books still doing so .

After what seemed a life time; a notice and a rail warrant arrived at my lodgings to report to the Recruiting office at Sheffield, in May 1946 I volunteered as A.C.H D.M.T for Five years .

I met Malcom Lee at Sheffield we were both joining up as Regulars in the trade of M.T. he was from Blackpool. After the initiation the same day sent to Pad-gate where we took the Kings Shilling and the Oath of Allegiance were given some of our Kit a ground sheet because it was Raining, this doubled up as a waterproof; a knife fork mug and spoon as we had to eat. During the visit to the Medical centre someone nicked my ground sheet. I Immediately following the earlier talks, this is your kit; You will be responsible for it; If you lose it you pay for the one you lost and the one to replace it. If someone nicks your kit, nick someone else's .

That was one of the first introductions into self-preservation, I took it and the first ground sheet that came available. I suppose with so many chaps milling around it was just a case of swopping kit .

Next day kit and all we were shipped off to Cardington R.A.F. station the old home of the Airships Enormous Hangers. We were to be the Ninth flight of a specialist training for the RAF, included in the regular square-bashing Drill, this we had to pass out at before going on to the station for the trade we were to follow. Was the drill now performed by the Queens Colour Squadron that we see today.
At the end of the day it was hoped to have not only a disciplined airman able to perform his trade, but also other duties prepared for during these months of training.

We were glad to be away from Padgate any way, it had a reputation of being a hard camp for the basic training, Cardington was near Bedford though no one was aloud out of camp for two weeks and then only if one could present the Uniform so as not to disgrace it, I Think we should have stayed at Padgate.
Number Nine Flight a row of four huts, Lorded over by a Flight Sergeant and four Corporal drill instructors, one corporal to each hut he lived in a small room at the end, about twenty beds in the hut and a pot-bellied stove and a Coal bin, never to be used it would dirty them. The Coal in this bin had to be taken out every week dusted and placed in uniform rows not only the top, the outside of this bin and some of the stove to be burnished using a small steel chain like

covered pad, the bright parts of the bayonet and scabbard the same and finally polished with the end of a spoon .

me

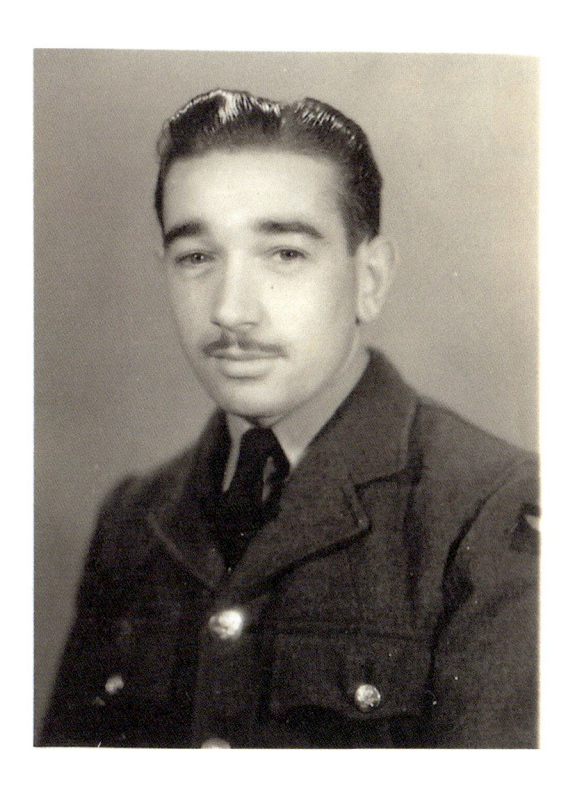

Boots the toe caps on issue were a mottled leather, these had to be burnished till they shone like patent leather also the Bayonet scabbard leather .
The floor was never walked on only by the flight Sergeant Corporal and inspecting Officer, we had to step from bed to bed to get to one's own bed space, when in the hut moving about one had two pieces of blanket to stand on and move by sliding ones feet. This floor shone like a mirror each hut was in competition to win points over the other three so there was no competition in the hut to slack off, one had the odd Muppet, but they spent much time on fatigue, it was less trouble to go with the flow. Personally, I would not have missed my time at Cardington for anything .

The bed space contained nothing that was not RAF property; or should not any way, one single Iron bed, three biscuits that made up the mattress a bolster same width as the mattress filled with straw. having been used so many times was as hard as wood, three blankets two sheets and a pillowcase .

Me far right

"At this time only, the RAF issued sheets not the Army." instructions were given how the bed space was to be kept, a small locker open fronted two shelves healed the regulation toiletries, a tall slim locker with door and inside one kit bag with regulation webbing small and large pack and spare pair of boots, also shining. Top shelf one overcoat and best blue folded in such a way to show the two buttons to the front, second shelf all one's underwear folded to a standard through the hut checked with a ruler on inspection," This was Discipline". Two rifles one for drill and one for firing, all had to be kept in a spotless condition .
The drill was the most important part to the drill instructors. In the morning after breakfast all outside in physical training kit and off to the square, back at the hut to change into uniform for rifle drill, and before one got through the door the corporal was screaming you should be outside by now, the drill included the now famous silent drill preformed now by the Queens Colour Squadron. A version of as on sentry go to the front quick march, we had lectures on all aspects of the other trades, Communications cooking unarmed combat and many other things. Sometimes dragged out at night to crawl about with blackened faces it certainly made a bunch of chaps work together .

One day the Padre gave a talk and asked if anyone was interested in communion lectures, I and another chap were interested and this was a very good move, any fatigue we may wish to avoid just to mention an engagement with the Padre was OK, it was easy to find something to see him about, that lasted most of my stay at Cardington. I was confirmed at St Al bans Cathedral.

It was four weeks into our service when the first pay parade took place, we stood for ages in the large hall and one by one names were called, one marched up to the pay table saluted gave number rank and name. If the paying officer was satisfied you signed for the two pounds, that was ten shilling a week, if not one waited until the last and tried again .
While all this coming and going in and out of the huts, the old bed space had to remain the same holy place, during the day and up until after tea, those biscuits that made up the mattress before first parade had to be placed one on top of each other, a pile of three. The three blankets inter spaced with the two sheets all folded to a given size throughout the hut, wrapped round with a blanket folded long wise, forage Cap on top the towel draped across the bed adorned with. One Mug knife fork and spoon, most of our spare time was spent polishing and cleaning. I never remember lying in bed one just got in fell asleep and woke up at the sounds of yelling," you lot going to stay there all day" At six thirty in the morning.

On the rifle range I maintained top score, my cooking task was to make the rice pudding for the whole flight at the rifle range, I don't know where it was, but we had to throw some Hand grenades,
 so, it must have been well out of the way. I used a lot of tinned milk a lot of sugar a lot of rice it must have been about two stone," it was all eaten" . The chap making the corn beef hash never got his fire going, it had to be eaten cold.

The final day came, passing out parade. We did not have our mummies come to watch like they do now, every belt was blanco'ed time and time again every button gleaming, socks pulled over boots to keep the shine until that moment when the Corporal screams out. "You should have been out side by now", the ammunition case on the rifle wedged out so it went in with a crack when struck with the palm of the hand during the general salute. It all went off very well no one wanted to be Re-flighted another month .
In the morning of the next day all the strict discipline seemed so far away , the Flight Sergeant and the Corporals were human beings again, as we lined up to be given our new posting and Railway warrant home for a week's pass.
Malcom and I were posted to RAF Weeton for a M.T. course .
My arrival at RAF Weeton was by the usual pick up from the Railway Station at Kirkham , by the MT routine run , at first one had to arrive , I know it sounds strange but to arrive one had to

sign in at all the departments one may use during the stay , also when leaving for another Station one had to be cleared by the reverse proses , one may be half way through an inoculation proses at the Sick quarters or was in possession of library books etc .

First one should arrive at the Mess and the bedding store having obtained the necessary forms from HQ , one has to Eat and sleep , The hut allocated by the section office according to whatever trade Course one was to take , tomorrow the rest of the arrival can be completed , The Course had not been given a starting date yet , one must find somewhere to hide apart from the hut , or work will be found for Idle hands , any section without exception the Cookhouse in need of extra hands would pounce on any Flight waiting course or posting , just after a mealtime was the fatal hour , outside our hut was a large Air Raid shelter just the place for an after lunch cigarette until the coast was clear , The most exciting thing in our life at the moment was sharing five woodbine and four cups of tea in the Naff I the day before payday .

After a week awaiting news of the course , we were told we were going Potato picking , on loan to some Farmers NR Chorley , About twenty of us by lorry arrived at Exton , a village outside Chorley to be housed in a hostel , it may have been for the Ammunition Factory that was only just up the road , we all had individual rooms with own wash basin and comfortable beds .

                        me

A home from home and very good food , our task was to go out to whatever Farm had requested our services , at the moment we were Government Surplus , The Farmers were using horse and Tractor drawn potato spinners we had to pick them up and put them into the potato sacks , quite a nice change from camp life , no one chasing one about , mind you I did find that a clip board with a few sheets of paper on it , one may walk all day about camp and no one would ask what you were about .

At most Farms there was plenty of tea and buns or sandwiches , they certainly liked there tea in Lancashire , at the end of the day a tip of two shilling or half a crown , some would not give at all saying" I am paying the RAF" for you lot .

There was not much for Entertainment sometimes we
would walk into Chorley to the Cinema , most nights one was only too glad to get into bed and sleep , not that we were all good boys you always get one , one day on the way to the farm stopping as we had been doing for some days at a certain shop , the shop full of men one or two helped themselves to the goods , they were seen and back on the truck it was expressed in no uncertain terms , the rotten thing to do just a small shop we all thought there would be more said about it , the next day the shop was closed the time we called , I expect the owners were not taking any more chances , just another example of a few Muppet's spoiling things for the rest .

One Farmer we had been working for the last two days when asked about the usual tip , and it was hard labour he had two spinners going, and before you had picked up the potatoes just spun out he was round again it was usual to get a little break between rounds , He said no I am paying the RAF for you lot and would not be persuaded otherwise .

Next day a chap from the Southern Counties he was a big lad but very gentle never hardly spoke to anyone , spent most of his spare time at the Farms with the Animals , put lots of the Chickens to sleep the old Farmer just smiled I expect he knew as I did how it was done , later he was not so sure when the ducks in the orchard and three tame rabbits in a wire pen were found to be dozing , Chickens yes ducks maybe , but never seen rabbits made to sleep , this was not all .

Later he gave us all a half crown each , the big lad said I expect he has found the pigs , there were two pens with four pigs in each all sound asleep , that was our last day at that Farm , and our last day potato picking , back at the hostel notice had arrived of the starting date of the MT course at Weeton

I often went back to that Hostel if I had a pass and in the Area I think it was a shilling a night with food , I do not know what happened to the big lad he failed the MT course and was re flighted to an Aerial erecting course , I expect he past his service time putting Sea Gull's to sleep on top of wireless masts , It was at Exton near the Hostel I met Tereasa later to become my first wife .

Now for the beginning of my trade as a Motor Transport Driver , though I had been driving for some years , now I had to learn to drive the way the RAF wanted it done , even long-standing Bus drivers had been known to fail the course .

The first day of the MT course started in the class room , the Instructor introduced himself and set out the general order of things , the first week is to be mainly in the class room , going through the rudiments of the vehicle , the highway code and the way the RAF dose things , for Instance , at all times with the exception of control movements , the hands shall be on the steering wheel in the position of ten to the hour and ten past the hour , the wheel to be turned by a push and pull movement , at no time will the hands be crossed , at all times the double clutch method will be used when changing gear , and the reasons as to why it should be done this way , a general grounding into what was expected of a RAF driver , to maintain safety to all concerned , all the mechanical and maintenance , details and theory and practical , a very thorough preparation before ever getting into a vehicle .

The second week we were allocated a vehicle , Hillman light car , three men and an Instructor to each vehicle , I had been able to drive since I was about ten years old , If it's there I want to know about it yet I had always had a mechanical aptitude .

Much later on as a mechanic I had developed a feeling mechanical of knowing a problem before laying a hand on a vehicle , I often wondered If I had a Guru by my side , sometimes these occurrences caused some wonderment , and not only to the Mechanical side of my life , on that subject and going back to the days cycling home from Melton , after late turn I had often a companion , a large black Dog , he joined me at the turning to High fields lane the Dr lives there now .
He trotted by my side and cut through just beyond the footpath to the left cutting through to the Lane's road , I thought nothing of It until one still night , It was obvious by its absence.

There was no noise from the feet , no usual clipping one gets as the claws touch the road , this dog virtually floated , I for some reason was not afraid , and the nights I did not see him , I missed him , strange but true , Mother have told me that I was borne at Chime hours .

The fact I was able to drive had no influence with the instructor , most of the chaps had some knowledge of the trade we were about to take , It was to be the RAF way or not at all , one chap was re flighted and had been a bus driver as a civilian , Each in turn we took the controls on the camp roads , and as soon as the instructor thought it was safe for us to be let loose on the main road , we were heading out to places like Garstang and Blackpool , on these light vehicles we trained for two weeks including the theory , the last day of the second week , a written test and a practical test with the senior driving instructor .

The next week was on the mid-range vehicle fifteen hundred weight Bedford truck , by now we had lost two chaps not being up to the required standard , this week was one of familiarization of the road and vehicle without the close scrutiny of the instructor , three trucks and one instructor in convoy , each trainee taking his turn at the wheel , at the end of the week there was no test , but a weekend pass , forty eight hour , I went back to the Hostel at Exton NR Chorley .

The next and final vehicle was a three ton Bedford , Theory again in the class room , some driving on the road , one instructor to three men and a vehicle , we also now returned after tea , for night convoy work and exercises how not to run over the dispatch riders , who were to keep the convoy all together but the best part was the supper , a normal supper was Cocoa and a large ship biscuit , the Cocoa was bitter and the biscuit very hard , our supper off the convoy , fried Bread and Egg Tea with lots of sugar , and one may have seconds , surly a feast fit for a King .

By now we were going into Blackpool with the QL trucks , mixing it with the Trams , a Cafe at the back of Blackpool football ground was one of our stops for break , I saw the team of the day in the Cafe , was able to get there Autographs , the team was in the local paper and I got them to Autograph the paper , I sold it that night in the Naff I for five shilling , Half a week's pay , at the time I was allowing mother a Shilling a day , that she was glad of .
Father was taking home under three pounds a week , so another seven shilling was quite a help .

The end of the final week , the final written examination , and off to Blackpool to meet the Civilian Driving Examiner , the RAF were not able to pass any one to drive on the Highway , therefore it had to be the Driving test Centre , I think there were six of us in the truck , and in turn took charge of the vehicle under instruction until told to stop and send round the next man .

After waiting all weekend , one had an Idea if one had satisfied the inspector yet waited with anticipation in the classroom on the Monday morning , as the instructor read out the course remarks and Test results , we were given our pink slip , this to go to our own licensing department , and the most cherished thing of all the yellow driving gloves , the mark of the MT driver , later comes the U boat Captains hat but that is another story .
Malcolm was posted to Weeton on permanent staff , he would be able to live at home his mother had a Hotel in Blackpool , I was posted to RAF Feltwell not so far from home , it was late Autumn and getting near to Christmas I hoped for this one at home .

At Feltwell I find the MT are in the same block as the Cooks and Police , modern housing a change to what I had been used to , the cook coming off nights would bring a bucket of tea to be brought around each bed space , you just dipped your mug in for that early cup of tea .

The police would have your pass before the time you were allowed to have it , the MT chap had knowledge of vehicle movements , so a useful collection of people all in the right place together , all worked unsocial hours anyway , one got used to the coming and going at all hours .

At the MT detail office was a civilian he detailed the jobs and runs and generally ran the section , later I found he was a prisoner of war , his name was Paul Telegman he had written it on his ruler that is how I knew , His English was implacable , there was a prisoner of war camp within the bounds of RAF Feltwell .

I worked some routine runs to the station , took stand by on the crash rescue tender at the flying control tower , also the Ambulance , we had a run with the spare Ambulance to Methwold to stand by when it was being used for flying by the Harvards , circuits and bumps , take off and landings .

Feltwell was a flying training school , we had a course from Canada finishing off there flying training , the change in the food caused many of the trainee pilots to go down with stomach problems , the Ambulance was busy at all hours going to RAF Ely Hospital .

I was sent to the sick quarters to relive the driver , later I moved into their little Nissan hut with the orderlies about six of us , the winter had set in and the trips to Ely getting less , I had more work from the MT detail office , and just before Christmas was told I may have a pass for the holiday , but on reporting back I was to go to Leconfield to bring back a refuelling tanker .

By the time I got away on my pass it was snowing , I got a lift into Mildenhall with the RAF routine run and hitched rides to Norwich and so on through to Corpusty , where the only ride I could get was on the trailer of a Tractor for most of the way , and walked the last few miles over the Snow .

I had with me at the time two medicine bottles of Navy Rum , It had been one of my tasks in the sick bay to issue the Rum for outside workers , one could go for your ration after breakfast , or after tea about two tots , I gave out half a Nafi cup each , the MT a little extra , during that time I had accumulated a few bottles , my arrival home was a little unsteady to say the least .

After Christmas back at the Orderly room I picked up the Rail warrant for Leconfield , I had not chanced the hitch hiking this time father had loaned me an old cycle , a single gear postman cycle , the snow was deep in places but keeping to the ruts I found it good traveling , In those days a second class ride was better than a first class walk .

leaving the cycle at the MT section I got the routine run to the station next day for Lecofield , arriving there was advised to wait until the roads had cleared , the tanker was wanted so I started the journey back to Feltwell , It took me three hours to get to Beverly I had then to skirt round the river Humber , the road was not too bad , some of the ruts were iced up and the tyres had been damaged , by the time I arrived at Sutton Bridge the tyre on the front gave up and burst in front of the Hotel , my luck was in the man who looked out to see what the noise was , much to my astonishment , was the Officer in charge of RAF Sutton Bridge , the camp was a little way down by the river embankment , he phoned them and I was able to get a bed for the night , And in the morning a spare wheel for the tanker and continue on my way .

Back at Feltwell the stocks of Coal were getting low , and lots of the other RAF stations who were closed for the cold spell had plenty , again I was detailed with two civilian drivers to collect there Coal we had three trucks a Studybaker a Doge and a Austin , as the Austin was a little cramped in the cab we were to take turns with each vehicle , with us in each vehicle were two POW from the POW Camp to help load the Coal , the snow was very bad but most days were able to get back before the mess closed , If we missed our late meal the POW camp found us a good meal .

The weather had improved and the station getting back to normal , I was helping back at the sick quarters again , the banks of the Dykes through the Southerly Fens were being lipped by water , the snow now causing more trouble as it was melting , at the time the Army had been called in to reinforce the banks , my brother who was in the Army was somewhere along the banks , I looked out for him but missed him , the Banks eventually gave way and the water flooded into the Fen .

I had been able to get through with the Ambulance but at Little port on return found I had to divert to Lakenheath , there were places where one could not see the road and hope not to run off it , on one of my later trips to Ely with the light Ambulance , I was able to get down to where the Army had camped , they were in Appalling conditions , there was nowhere dry to stand let alone sleep , the only food they had was some Fish and chips the young Officer had to commandeer at the local fish shop , and pay for them himself , I was able to see my brother for a while I left what few shillings I had in my pocket , this was the winter of 1946 : 1947 .

Later another ferry job to Weeton Ash-ton to bring back another Ambulance , this time I flew by Harvard , we flew over the floods of the Fens and only then could one see the devastation that had been caused , the RAF camp at Aston was deserted with the exception of a few sheep , that had to be scared off by a low pass , I picked up the Ambulance and started my journey back , I had a letter to post home and a very strange thing happened on the way , I remembered the letter and on the lookout for a post box , all of a sudden I knew that the long green well clipped hedge I was passing had a Post Box set back into the hedge , I posted my letter , many of the roads had yet to have the sign posts replaced , I had little idea where I was other than somewhere on the road to Leicester , I had never been to Ash by DE La Zouch , the interesting thing was they thought it was near the sea .

The Yanks had a song , Ashby De La Zouch by the sea .

How did I know so positively that Post Box was where I found It , that was the interest that brought my mother's notice to the letter again ?

The spring was not far away the orderly room sent for me . Another posting , RAF Mamby , another chap named Starman from Norwich was to go with me , much later my mother had a letter from his parents that he had Died , well it will be Summer by the Sea side .
I arrived at RAF Mamby not quite with a bang. The explosion was from a little man with a Tate and Lyle syrup label on his wrist. " The SWO". I was about to cross the square to the billet.

I was told that was the one the MT were using, He called out with a voice that could shatter glass. Making remarks about crossing; "Hallowed ground". No! one walked over the parade ground at Mamby. Let alone a U boat Captain; said he Making remarks about my cap. It was practice for the MT drivers to obtain a; Peaked cap take out the wire that makes it flat on top, line the inside of the rim with a thick rope; and with a thick piece of card support behind the badge the front stood up, and the sides drooped over. Like the man said a "U boat Captain".

Go the long way around he said; that I done and very quickly. By the time I got to the billet he was nowhere in sight, I was thankful for that; now sweating from toil and fear; loaded as I was made haste the security of the Block.

I must have scared him off. The hat stayed out of sight during my stay at Mamby.

I was lucky ; could have received at least seven days C.B. That was worse than it sounds. For the seven days one has to report to the Guard room every morning before Revile in full webbing. That is small pack, large pack, water bottle, all attached to the webbing straps, with the brass gleaming, and dressed in best "Blue Uniform". For the raising of the Ensign, and after work the same procedure at the guard room followed by camp fatigues, usually cleaning the cooking utensils in the cook house, or some other ridiculous task like painting the grass green; around the parade ground where it was brown due to the sun. Prisoners today get better treatment for Murder.

It was not long before I came to the conclusion, this was going to be no home from home. An Officers training School., Even the MT had to parade once a week for AOC's parade "and with Guns". Unheard of in most Stations. They keep the MT out of the way, they smell of oil and diesel and cannot March.

Still there is always the notice board, the jobs that need volunteers. This is a case where the saying No one Volunteers for anything is proved wrong.

I get a few routine jobs that take me off the camp. I drove the Cricket team bus ; even though it entailed Saturday afternoons as well. One afternoon the fan belt broke in Louth smashing the Distributor to pieces, not much seemed to go right there. The meal wagons a Standard van; that stank like nothing on Earth. The duty run with it was to the Cookhouse pick up the meals for the Sick bay and the guard room, I stopped in a hurry; the lot came up the front with me.
"I had been watching the notice board". I Volunteered for a hair cutting course. I was getting Desperate to leave Mamby. I tried Mountain Rescue and Summer camp attachment; anything that would get me away from all this Bull.

One of my visits to the AOC's Villa for his car, I found the Batman working for the AOC was Bob Cushions from Briston a pleasant surprise, later he came up to the billet and we had quite a chat.

I was called to the orderly room. "Now what have I done?". However, Fear Not. A posting to Driffield for the ATC summer camp. At last I am free for the time being.

At Driffield a bed space was found for me in the MT billet, though we would have no connection with the MT. Over the road was a Tented site already in place, rows of four-man tents and a marque. We collected our vehicles, a Dodge and an Austin for trooping, a Beverett for taking the tow out to the Glider. I forget what type that was, and a winch that had seen service with some Balloon section.

The staff were; One officer who we saw little of, a sergeant he was to instruct the N.C.O.'s cadets in drill, and ourselves two drivers, to drive the trucks and help with the Glider.

We met the train at the Station, and the first attachment arrived on to the site. It was now our duty to show them how to fill up the paillasses with straw to make up the bedding for their tents. This was supposed to be done with each new intake. We had better use for all that straw, the sergeant had made friends in the village with some people that had a Horse riding stable, and in return for the straw we were able to go horse riding as often as we could get away

I did not mind that, I was able to ride without falling off, for a short while I was away at Bridlington with the Air Sea Rescue boats, I was not too keen on the noise from the Engines and glad to get back to the camp.

It came to a close with a visit from the Canadian Air Cadet force. A Grand party was put on for them at Skegness. In the Spar, it was there last camp before returning to Canada. Having been on a tour of the United Kingdom we cleared the camp and returned to our respective Stations.

At Mamby I was redirected to Weeton again, for a DMTM course. Now I had to learn to repair them as well as drive them. This I think was the beginning of the new Technician trades, another experiment by the powers that be.

In that trade one would never become a LAC but SAC, no longer the cry. LAC one GC do not try to bull shit me. LAC . GC, a converted position, somewhat like a WO, though very far apart. He avoids the things that fall upon the other ranks, he avoids the chores of the NCO's. Like a lost soul ; I did later achieve that position, so back to Weeton.

At Weeton the course was billeted down in the old five wing huts, they were so bad the place was passed over by any inspection. The huts stood on stilts what was left of them; some had been sawn off and used for fire wood, to keep the hut fire going.

In the classroom to each two trainees. I will not say Students because we were to be taught and learn something at the end of the course, was an Enfield Cub Diesel Generator. We were taught the theory and the practical side of the trade.

And sometimes at lunch break the Engines would have been tampered with by the instructor, and on returning to class he would say. Start your Engines, it was up to us to find the fault and get the Engines going. I found the course a very happy six weeks.

I had many pleasant weekends at Blackpool. I rather liked going into the tower ball room and listing to Reg Dixon play the Organ . All the Tower was free to service men, so it was a cheap outing. There was not much of a fun Fare there then, but a few sideshows and pin ball machines. And the Laughing Policeman. I would think he is the longest attraction there today.

All good things come to an end we finish the course and await posting.

During that time, I developed a Diesel rash, I reported sick, the Medical Officer sends me home on sick leave for two weeks, within the two weeks it clears up and I report back to Weeton. Only to be told I have been reported missing. The sick bay had made the arrangements for my sick leave and not informed the Orderly room, who wanted me for Embarkation leave.

I had been reported missing, so the Guard room had to hold me until it was all cleared up, that did not take long and next day I was off home again on a week's Embarkation leave. I report to Burtonwood for overseas posting.

At Burtonwood we are issued with the overseas Kit bag and the tropical uniform, that was Khaki drill shorts and uniform, the Insignia was in red and the Eagle on the shoulders, a tin plate and sun glasses the pith helmet was out now, the powers that be having decided, one gets Sun stroke through the Eyes not the head.

All the Injections signed for and we one early wet morning are taken to the Railway station and to the port of Southampton. I had by now; I would not say pal, but a chap who seemed to be going the same way as I most of the time. His name was Hempstead.
He came from London, I never knew his Christian name he answered to the name Happy we trooped on board our Mummies did not come to see us off, we were to be away for three years, we would not get any Counselling. More like the glass house should we get up sett.

Leaving Southampton Happy said They say the Bay of Biscay is bad and every one will be sick, but he added I have been told if you keep walking and eating it will be ok, we found it a good pastime to try to walk the deck in a straight line on the rolling deck, there was not much to do. Happy soon found out how to earn a few pennies. Early in the mornings he would buy a jug of tea from the Galley and sell it for a penny a mug to those still in their bunks, we were about one Hundred RAF and bunked in the deck lounge.

This was one of the Castle lines a passenger ship called the" Arundel Castle". Quite a large vessel, the Army chaps were below decking there were allot more of them, and I understand in hammocks and closed down in rough weather. We watched the waves running from the Bow to the Stern the height of the waves was unbelievable at times, in calmer water we saw the porpoise swimming in front of the ship. Over the stern at night the Phosphorescence in the water changing as the rise and fall of the ship caused the propellers nearing the surface to take down air. We Experienced the vibration of the shaft at the stern, the cells were there and as two RAF chaps were in cells for some misdemeanour, we had to take turns guarding them. I only took one turn thank goodness.

The Royal Marine band were on board and gave concerts ; during good weather.

After what seemed weeks we arrived at Malta, and steamed into Valleta Harbour, lots of little boats came along side selling things, buckets lowered on string brought up the goods, it became somewhat of a fiasco. Some of the goods were not paid for, some paid for goods they did not get, in the end the local police came, those who did not leave were thrown into the water.

Next day we Sailed for Port Said we had seen it all before now; and the journey was getting tedious, it was very hot and still March. Not much could be found for so many chaps to do, Happy and I found odd jobs cleaning in the mess we used, thinking; we can choose what we do rather than be detailed off for other tasks that no one wanted. In time we arrived at Port Said.

We were leaving the Ship before breakfast so nothing to eat for us. Standing on the dock side waiting for the train to take us down the Suez Canal to Ismallia and the camp RAF El'Hamra.

A green van that had been for some time just over from the Railway track. Opened up its side, Two Smiling faces holding up cups of tea and buns. " The Salvation Army", they were always there when needed most and in no time handed out nearly one hundred cups of tea and a bun, from that little green van.

We were herded rather than marched over to the train, just wooden seats and open carriages, everyone was warned not to leave anything they did not want to lose near the windows, even then one chap had his wrist watch slashed off his wrist without so much as a scratch to his arm. At every stop the venders did not seem to get any less, running up and down the train trying to sell things, one chap was very noticeable, he was really black and would call out. I am" Jock Mc' Gregor from Scotland", they were climbing on to anything they could get hold of and riding to the next stop, even on top and some under the train. I do not know the most the Flies or vendors.

[me]

At last we stopped at Ismallia and taken on to El'Hamra RAF site by truck. This was March 1948 and I was to have my 21 St birthday in a tent. Tent No 35; Camp 1, RAF El'Hamra MEF, at that time it cost mother six pence to send the first letter I received from her since leaving in January.

Today I would have been counselled and sent home with an enormous compensation. El'Hamra and waiting for a posting, it is Sand as far as the Eye can see.

Life in the tent is quite pleasant, little chaps run past with another tent on their backs only to have some fool put his foot out and over they go. I wonder why they carry those little tins of water about with them. Obviously, something to do with their toilet.

We place ammunition boxes full of sand around the tent to keep the tent fly sheet down on the ground there can be quite severe storms at this time of year we are told.

At the start of each day those awaiting posting parade on a clear plot of sand called the parade ground not much to indicate what it is, just more sand. The first to parade are the civilian workers, Arabs they make up the tents; clean up the camp and keep the place generally tidy. They cannot trust themselves to keep working, they employ a "Task Master" to keep them in line and pay him from their own wages. Good jobs are hard to come by in the Canal zone. The first time I saw them being given the days orders I thought. This tall black chap was standing on a box he stood head and shoulders above the rest, I believe his cast was Sudanese, he had a whip and used it.

[me]

On the first parade of the day if your name was called you reported to the orderly room, it may be for a posting or some other duty, If it was cigarette day you joined the queue passing between two beds on the parade ground, handing out from one side a tin of fifty Players, from the other boxes of matches, the matches were not only to light the cigarettes, but your little oil lamp in the tent, the one you made the day you received your blankets, out of a cigarette tin and piece of wick having filled it with paraffin and found out after all you could not use it because, if it was high enough to give any light at all it filled the tent with smoke. We were told to put the legs of the bed into ones boots, that if they were being stolen at least you would see them go, also to sleep with the arm across one's chest hand placed on the shoulder, then any attempt to put a string around your neck, it would end up under your armpit hopefully. One was well informed that the locals often strayed into the Camp and could take the sheet away from under you without any disturbance.

The food was good, at breakfast you took your own tin plate knife fork and spoon, if the water outside the mess, normally a large tank heated by the steam from the kitchen boiler; was out of order you rubbed the utensils in the sand to clean them, Lunch was at mid-day, it was called Tiffin, usually collected and taken back to the tent, great care must be taken to cover ones plate, especially if it contained any meat, those Vultures known as shite hawks, could come from out of nowhere and take your meat in a flash.

From midday on no one worked unless they really had to, tea or dinner was at about four, then some work again in the evening if you had any to do, we were not supposed to leave the camp, but it was only a short walk through the village of kasfareet to the bitter lakes, where a place had been wired off to keep the Sharks out and we could swim, after a swim in those waters the salt dried on the skin like white powder.

One morning many names were called. Also, Happy and I. At the orderly room we were given our posting, most of those on the Ship with us to go to Aden in the Red Sea. Happy and I were for RAF Hasani in Greece; and The RAF Delegation in Athens. The next day not long after the main body had left for Aden news came through the train had been blown up by the Stern Gang. Partisans of some unknown cause; to us any way. Most of them were killed.
Little did I realize, when I landed in Egypt those early days of 1948. "A Civil War was in progress". Surly the War Office had not sent me to do something about it? I had been given a Rifle, but no ammunition. I was under the Impression it was one of the ways the government transported, "Alms to North Africa" and was sure of having someone responsible for them. We were told that if it was lost, we would have to pay for a new one also the one lost, that alone ensured It never left my side.

After a Train ride down the banks of the Suez Canal we, my comrades and me. There were one Hundred of us RAF personnel. Not far from the Bitter Lakes. The RAF Station. EL. Hamra M.E.F.

There were allocated a tent in, Camp 1. Tent Nr 35. Given a tin of fifty Players and told. "This is your lamp", three pools and six blocks of wood with a hole in each, and three hard square biscuits. "This is your bed", "three blanket's", the man said. "It is a waste of time giving sheets, the Arabs nick them from under you while you are asleep, and by the way" he remarked, "put the legs of the bed in your boots or they will have them as well. Sleep with your arm across your throat and hand on the opposite shoulder that way it is more difficult for them to strangle you". "What! about the lamp" I said."! OH yes" the man said. "You Smoke the fags, make a hole in the lid of the tin, put a piece of string through the hole put in some paraffin, if you can stand the smoke you will have a reasonable light in the tent, by the way we are due for some heavy rain and wind, better get some Ammunition boxes filled with sand to hold the tent down". As a parting gesture he said. "Parade on the square at eight thirty in the morning for instructions".

EL.Hamra was just a stepping off Camp to wherever we were to be posted. The food was good, breakfast at seven thirty to eight thirty, Tiffin (light snack) at Twelve, tea at four, and dinner at eight. Work stopped for most at twelve, and started again from five to eight or thereabouts, depending what work one was engaged in. I realized then why, "The Song, Mad dogs and English-men go out in the Midday Sun. No one worked in the heat of the Midday

Mostly if one's name was not called out for Fatigues or (Posting), meaning they wanted to be parted from your company to some other field. I was only Detailed Guard duty once. Twelve to four at the M.T. Gate. I had one of those Apprentice boys, from Cranwell as a companion guarding the gate. We had been given five rounds of ammunition, that was very comforting; though the Guard Sergeant did say. "If you fire one of those rounds you will have to account for it.

Having taken to heart the warnings of our initial lecture about the possible enemy. I positioned myself behind the M.T. guard house that was closed; but had a comfortable seat out of site of the man on the nearby tower, who constantly swung the beam of his light over the gate lighting the two of us up. My comrade having been drilled in guard procedure, said "You know old man it's just not Cricket. One's not allowed to keep out of sight". However, he did see my point when I outlined the possibilities that the Enemy did not see it that way and would not hesitate to remove us from the gate to gain admission at whatever cost it would take.

The Enemy! I thought the war was over, however a Civil War had been raging since 1940. "The Stern Gang". Fighters for the freedom of Israel. A Zionist Guerrilla group founded by. Abraham Stern carried out Anti-British attacks, During the U.K. Mandate rule in Palestine. Both on individuals and strategic targets. Stern was killed by British Forces in 1947. The group survived until 1948. With the Creation of the independent State of Israel. In February 1948 the Stern gang Blew up a train carrying British Soldiers from Cairo to Haifa; Killing 27 of them also many of the RAF personal who were in the posting with me to M.E.F. One of our chaps who was badly injured had recently re-joined the Service finding civilian life was not all the Government had promised. He had been in the Arnham Parachute drop during, W.W.2 without a scratch only to have his life shattered by a band of renegades.

We had time to visit him in Fayed Hospital before my posting to Athens was announced. Would you believe it.? Landing in Greece and taken to Athens Where I am to take my place in the M.T. company. I find Greece is in the middle of a Civil War, that started in 1946 and ended in 1949.

Holding my post at the finishing of booth conflicts. I can assure you I had nothing to do with the success on either count.

   Though being the inquisitive type I tried to understand the reason for the conflicting differences.

During 1941 to 1944 the German Occupation of Greece. Rival Monarchist and Communist groups from 1942. A Communist- dominated resistance movement, Armed and trained a Guerrilla Army, and after W.W.11, the National Liberation front as it was called, wanted to create a Socialist State. If the Greek Royalist Army had not had a massive assistance from the USA and Great Britain

this undoubtedly would have happened.

   The Civil War ended when the Royalists defeated the Communists, and the Monarchy was re-established until 1967 when Government conflicts between the King and his Ministers, resulted in a Coup Replacing the Monarchy with a new Regime.

Personally, I Sympathise with the National Liberation front, after all they were the ones who stood up to the German occupation as a Guerrilla Force.

   As for myself my part in the whole affair was not very exciting, RAF life carried on as always though living and working in the City surrounded with more Civilians than RAF personnel was to say the least different. I encountered a quantity of High Explosive hidden in one of the vehicles I was servicing, leading to a rapid attack on the Garage (My work place in Athens) by our own special investigating branch of the RAF Police, rather more alarming than had it been the resistance movement.

   One other encounter happened as I was driving the AOC to work, I had now been moved to the Villa outside Athens, my duty as driver to the Air Officer Commanding RAF personal advising the Monarchist in their conflict. We were stationed in a Villa at Varkiza near Vouliagmeni about ten miles outside Athens. It is now a children's Home. This I was told by one of my Amateur radio contacts recently, his home is at Vula close to the Villa.

   We had just arrived at the junction of Leof Vasil, there I usually took the left turn to get round behind the Tammion buildings, (The headquarters of all Military personnel), this way enabled me to drive up to our parking place behind the Admiral and the General's car enabling the AOC to embark from the car on to the pavement; directly in front of the entrance. However this morning a traffic jam ahead of us, Police waving their arms in the air pistols drawn, I explained in my pigeon Greek to the face in the car window that I must go through and pointed to the Flag flying on the car bonnet, he just threw his hands in the air, with the expression that only said Mad Englishman; stepped to one side as I made my way along the pavement and round the corner, at that moment I realized what all the fuss was about, Explosions and small arms fire to my right. The Guerrilla Army were throwing grenades and firing small alms at the "Grand Breton". A large Hotel used mostly by visiting service officers. The AOC looking over the top of his paper just said. "Drive on Driver", by the time I had arrived at the front of the building it was all over.

  The only other occasion was, we had just seated for lunch at the villa in the staff dining room, when it came one of the houses maids. Quick Johnny Bandits spirit away all master's washing off the line outside, we decided to look into that after lunch, when hopefully they will have moved well away.

  Things were relatively quiet by the time my three years were up, though in the earlier days the Villa staff included six full time Greek guards, Two RAF drivers, the cars were one Humber Pullman, one Humber Snipe, "That was my car", one RAF Cook, one RAF Batman, one Greek Cook, one Greek Maid, and two Greek Gardeners. I left in 1950 flew home with Sir Auther Henderson, Secretary of State, "for Air" (I did not mix as you can see with any old Hoy! Paloy). Tolly who had just rejoined the RAF he was an ex Parachute Regiment and had been at the Arnham drop. I understand he was sent back to the UK later, from the hospital in Fayed, a few days later Happy and I left for Athens by RAF Dakota we flew over the Lybyan desert to EL'Adam a one-time Y station; Radio Intelligence after a short stay we left for RAF Hassani and Athens.

We landed at Hassini now Athens Airport. Then it consisted of two wooden huts. RAF Hassani the main RAF Station .

They looked after our Delegation Aircraft two Ansons. Happy and I were taken to the HQ in Athens on the main street.
The Tammion building, the RAF Delegation consisted of about twenty Airmen and about fifteen Officers.

The Delegation was a group of Officers Nco's and Airmen . The Army and Navy were also represented. Their task was to advise the Greek forces in their Confrontation with the Enemy. Greece was trying to quell a hostile Force under General Markos, or like sounding name, later this was recorded as the Hidden War.

The Greek Government issued a Decoration for those serving there. The War office refused the Decoration at the time.

Apart from some activity around the area near to the HQ buildings and; The Camp fires of the Partisans in the Ymetos hills, a troop of horseback riders pursuing the AOC's car one day on the road to Larisa; the disappearance of food and clothing from the Villa. There was not much seen of the Enemy that bothered us.

I was found a bed in the SIB billet, they; had some going begging, not surprising not everyone wanted to live with the Special Investigation Branch of the RAF Police.

Happy had moved into the mess another large private house a few blocks up the street, It had a large palm tree in the garden at the rear, I burnt it down one day trying to start a truck the tin of petrol I was using to fill the carburettor caught fire, I threw it out and on to the dead palm leaves and up it went like a fiery torch; not the last of my fires. I had taken charge of a Chevrolet three-ton wagon, it was filthy. one night it was too hot to sleep, I got up and with some rags and cleaning materials proceeded with the light from an oil lamp to clean the cab, the fumes from the cleaning material caught alight, and I was lucky to get out of the cab without getting burnt. Another chap who was up after trying many fire extinguishers that did not work was able to find one that did and put out the flames.

It was a Corporal Williams I remember well. It was also the fact that most of the fire extinguishers not working was the reason the whole Incident was hushed up by the fire department. Later I was able to get a bed up in the Delegation Garage.

A large Bus Garage out of town on the Thessalonica road. Its last occupants had been the Gestapo of the German Army. They had left a blue Mercedes car behind a certain Group Captain laid claim to it. Opposite was a small Cafe " Taverna" ran by an old man and his wife they had a son Paul.

Paul brought the Tea and snacks over to the workshop for us; he also showed where the Hostages had been shot in the garage by the Germans.

I was now doing the Salvage run, and the Ice run, and looking after the Electrician shop. Being the only DMTM the task was mine, also any mechanical repair that may come up. The Salvage run was from the Unit collected once a week and taken to a dump out by Varkisa. This dump was inhabited by a few families, the lived on the dump and off the refuge that was taken there.

The flies were so thick the wipers had to be running all the time to keep the window clear. The Ice run was once every three to four days; all the Airmen living away from town had Ice boxes to keep food fresh. I picked up the Ice from a Brewery along the Mad Mile "Singro Avenue" The road from Athens to Piraeus; It was called FIX'S Brewery. They also made an Ice Cream "Surprise" Fancy that .

I also drove the Coles Crane and Diamond T wrecker if needed, and the Bus up to Mount Parnis and to Voiliagmenis beach for swimming.

In our off times we visited the Acropolis and the Lykavittos this was a little church on a very high hill could be called a small mountain, the path up was just behind the Airman's mess. At Easter time from the Acropolis one could watch the lighted candles procession moving from town centre all the way up to the Lykavittos and down again.

I often wondered what the partisans were doing at the time, more than likely in the procession. During the hot times we slept on the flat roof, a Cinema was just over the road an open air one and one could watch from one's bed.

At the time I was sending home parcels of fruit It was cheap and on ration in the UK. After things quietened down the threat to the Greek Government was over and our services no longer needed, we started to move all the equipment out and back to Egypt.

The AOC sent for me would I stay up at the Villa as one of his drivers was leaving for the UK. Two drivers one cook and a batman seem like a happy little family.
At the villa we had two cars, a Humber Pullman and a Humber Snipe, my car was the Humber Snipe.

The cook and I had a caravan in the Villa grounds, the other driver and the batman had rooms in the Villa staff quarters. Our duty as drivers was one day on and one off, the day on was to take the AOC into Athens. The office was in the Tammion building. All senior staff had offices there.
The routine for the day. The first important job of the day was; wash Shave and breakfast served by the civilian cook in our Quarters.
Back in my Caravan, that was parked next to the Service cook's Caravan, my uniform, Karki drill having been all pressed for the day; by the villa staff lay out on my bed. However, the Car needs to be prepared and polished. having done that, I may get myself dressed for the day; taking care to present the uniform to the A.O.C. to his approval.

Having taken the Car to the main entrance opened the passenger door; Saluted as he gets in passing a look over my Uniform.
"We are the Junior Service "I unfurl the Ensign on the front of the car and drive away for the headquarters in Athens. Arriving at the Tammion building the H.Q. had to park outside in pecking order, Navy Army and Air Force, take off the Ensign from the front of the car and go to the P.A. office read the diary for the days Official duties, find the way to the various destinations, and who was to be there.

Again, pecking order to be observed, must not arrive after the senior service. If Royalty to be present it is fatal to be behind them, the senior arrives last and leave first. Sometimes the day ended with a dinner, so at times the day was a long one; and mostly hanging about waiting. One soon got to know the drivers of the other officials, and where to go to the rear of the residence in question and were duly lavished with food and drink.

My first day on arriving at the office the AOC looking through the office door, said Would you mind going down to the Delegation Garage and take the Ensign down. Someone had left it flying, I did just that and put it in my kit bag, it is now with the Muckle Bough Collection at Weybourne. They have a Radio shack there and quite a few items of service Exhibits.

All the bulk of the service men in Athens had gone; either back to the UK or to Egypt. We were part of the Diplomatic force now. Flying the Flag as one may say.
.
On the day off there were the Villa duties to see to, take the drinking water vehicle for filling, the only water available was from a very deep Well, being very near to the sea it was salty. Take away the salvage. If the Lady of the Villa wanted to go out that was another job, if we had Official High-Ranking visitors. The Pullman car was at their disposal, the Snipe to take the Lady's out and about. Most wanted to go to Corinth and Sunion, both quite long trips, and into Athens to see the shops. Sometimes an official function, would end with a dinner at the official residence. The ladies had to arrive just as their husbands.

Air staff were going in; and it was quite a problem to get them into the correct pecking order. The driver of official cars had quite a responsible task.

We had visits from Royalty at the Villa. Everyone had to be vetted days before hand, the villa grounds alive with armed guards, a job to get to the toilet without being searched, often a dinner party was staged at the villa. I always got the job of making the Ice cream, after lunch I would have go to Fixes Brewery for the Ice. Get out the cream tub; a box within a box. The cook brings down to the cellar the mixture and put it into the centre box, my job now is to keep forcing ice in between the two boxes and keeping the holes clear to let the water out. Eventually the Ice cream is ready. From the kitchen it is served with HOT chocolate, after all my work then to pour a hot chocolate over it; to me seems rather pointless.

From the Villa we could look out over the grape vine field to the sea. The AOC had a small boat, we may use it but not the Engine. "That the Canadian Ambassador had loaned him" . So, we made a sail for it. A" Lateen sail". We had seen the Greek boats with them, and it sailed very well, often at times off duty we sailed up and down the bay.

At Hassani we had two Anson Aircraft. The AOC flew himself he had been a bomber pilot. I always went with him; If he was visiting up North. We lost one of the Anson's; the PA took some business up north, the Navigator wanted to come backs that night his wife was expecting; they took a chance and found a Mountain in the cloud booth were killed. P/O Redmain from Norwich and Navigator W/O Bardoe. they are buried in the Military Cemetery just outside Athens. I do not know the reason for the crash; the AOC was very upset I can see him standing in the door to our dining room now, telling us of the accident. The A.O.C. was a short man with a moustache His home had been in Canada originally. A French Canadian I was to understand.

The job of a high-ranking officer is a lonely one. If he tells his junior officers a joke, they always laugh he once told me, at times it is helpful to have one's decisions questioned. Rarely dose this happen, so I expect it was of some light relief to have a broad Norfolk driver who just said what comes naturally. We had a position of trust and what we heard and saw we kept to ourselves. I used to wear American Silk KD shirts and long trousers silk black tie. "Seldom shorts", patent leather shoes. All to be frowned upon by any respectable Drill Sergeant.

The new PA arrived and was in the office when I was checking the Diary for the day. I wondered what all the shouting was about. Until I realized he was talking to me. I had not saluted him what was I doing in his office he was still storming away when the door opened from the AOC's office and he beckoned to the PA come in.

The door closed but I did catch the words. You leave my drivers discipline to me. I never heard any more about it.
I had been out on one of my days off with the boat, called in at a Taverna and must have eaten something that was bad or had been bitten by a fly or booth. Later and at night I awoke and was only able to get to the caravan steps. The cook found me as he was up early for duty, he raised the other driver who got the A.O.C. up; to send for the Army M/O.

The A.O.C insisted I was taken into the Villa and put to bed there. The M/O came said I had Malaria and Dysentery and should go into the BMH, but the AOC's wife was not having that. I was to stay in the Villa under her Care. She was my nurse for three weeks, and personally saw to my well-being.

By the time I was walking about again, my tour of duty was well over the A.O.C had been saying he must get me transport back to the UK soon.

The Secretary of State Sir Arthur Henderson was visiting Athens and the Villa he agreed to take me back with him in his Aircraft.

Athens was now behind me. Dakota KN647 at 8,5oo feet Pilot Lt Hayman, Navigator Flt J.G.Burgh at the ground speed of 155 miles per hour.

Transport Command; now I think it's called The Queens Flight. Heading out over the Mediterranean Sea, and for Malta. At Luqa the Secretary of State left he Aircraft through a line of Guards to the Welcoming committee.

During this time, I stayed In the Aircraft out of the way. No one knew who I was, I do not think they wanted to ask outright, and I was not saying. So, I was given the Red-carpet treatment, to the Mess and a bed for the night, and Informed a Car would pick me up in the morning to take me to the Aircraft.

I found the Naafi for the Evening and in the morning was taken to the Aircraft.

The next part of the journey was still over the Mediterranean Sea and Niece, the South of France ; the sands were covered with Bathers as the Aircraft came in low to land. The landing strip must have been quite close to the water. It was the same as before only this time it was Gendarmes who lined the path from the Aircraft.

I was Ushered out at the rear of the party and moving up with them to the welcoming party. When! the ward master off the Aircraft came up behind and discretely guided me out to the right of the guards, saying I expect you would like some lunch. As it was dinner time I said Yes, and we had a very nice meal and returned to the Aircraft.
The stay was not long. I expect only a stop off for lunch. It was Evening as the White Cliffs came into sight and we landed at RAF Northolt.

The Secretary of State was whisked away. As for me again the officer in charge was taking no chances Who was this ERK with the S of S What! did I require he said. Somewhere to sleep and some Fish and Chips Sir I remarked.

I had promised myself that. He took me to a Billet told one of the occupants to find me a bed and to direct me to the local Chip shop just off camp. In the morning I reported to the orderly room and explained who I was.

Yes, the Sergeant said you have been having a few people guessing since you left Athens, a Corporal Jackson with a S.A.C. Propeller seemed to have caused some confusion. Well they only had to ask I replied. He then told me there was a Car to take me to somewhere in London for Debriefing.

There I was taken half way up a tall building and in a very nice room was given Tea, and two Civilian gentlemen sat opposite me and started to ask all about my stay in Athens.

How I liked working on the Delegation what were my Hobbies how did I get on with the A.O.C. and so on. They remarked that it was a special kind of duty in a special situation and needed a special kind of person to fill the post. They asked. Where I would like to be posted to, I said RAF Marham that was near to home.

They both shook hands with me saying the car will take you to RAF West Drayton. You can dispose of your tropical kit and they will arrange for your posting to Marham.

RAF West Drayton. now life as I had known it, stopped just there. At the Guard Room a big Flight Sergeant came sliding forward on two pads of felt so as not to mark the polished floor. I was dragging one of two kit bags. A large pack over my shoulder, and the old U boat Captains Hat was back in its rightful place. He was getting redder and redder.

Out from the gloom came another one. I thought it's the Cells for me. But no; fate was holding out; it was a Familiar face from the past. After a few words the big one left and the new found friend helped to sort out all the details that would remove me of my excess baggage. That! I was now told I should have left over there any way. It was one of the ways they have of getting kit over there yet having someone responsible for it all the time.

This Flight Sergeant was one from the SIB billet in Athens; he had come home same time as I moved up to the Villa.

I had not realized my Fame had travelled so far. It was he who came to the garage at Kifisia to question me when I had found the Explosive charge from a very large Shell in the locker on a vehicle I was repairing.

It was Destined for the Enemy; I had unsuspectingly waylaid it, put it in the compound that I was using as the Electricians workshop. Used some of it to make Insulation washers for the contact breakers of that vehicle. We had a good chuckle about all that, he found me a bed and after two days I was able to get cleared and away off home on leave, with the instructions to report to RAF Marham at end of leave.

At RAF Marham The Quarters are now modern housing blocks, still a dormitory sleeping arrangement now heated and much better Ablutions.

The MT was No 1 Hanger up Lady Wood end of the Camp. I am detailed to drive the Camp Commanders car, after one trip out with it I reported it unfit to go on the Highway.
There was quite a rumpus in the maintenance section no fault was apparent, yet I insisted it was unstable on the road. It was; and it had to be driven every inch of the way, I suspected the Caster Angle was out. If the Caster Angle was in order one should be able to let go of the steering wheel after turning it and it should take up a straight-ahead position, this did not .

The flight sergeant said it was ok, in the end the post was given to another driver who would not complain.

This was the same on the Breast Sands run. At the Bombing Range we had to transport the spotters, these were men from the Armour y. Their job was to set sight on the bombs dropped in practice Bombing at a range Nr the Wash. I drove them as far as I thought safe along the Sea Defence bank.

A very high bank with a very narrow road on top. One day with a new Armoury Officer with the party insisted, I drove further along to be near the observation post. I refused he threatened me with all sorts of punishment I would not budge. Next day he wanted another Driver.

I think it took them a week to get the truck back up from the marsh, the other Driver had done as the Officer told him and rolled the truck down the bank.

I was now driving the Married families Bus in from Sutton Bridge; it was a very early start to get out to Sutton Bridge pick up the living out personnel and be back at Marham for just before

Eight. I did not mind I was in my last year. I had dropped My Honorary Stripes, being a Technician by trade the LAC was of the other none Technical Airmen rank. Having just been awarded the GCB I was now entitled to wear the stripe at the wrist and the three-blade propeller, not quite as the old song would have it; but one extra blade.

A coveted position by the old hands. Some did not make it; some went up too far and missed it, no one bothers him, young Airmen and some unsuspecting ones Salute him.

A bit of an odd man out. I do not think he exist anymore in the Service.

I have now a Coles Crane to look after as well. A few jobs unloading at the Railway Station Narbough I done a few private lifts at the Maltings I think it was in Narbough. The Boss gave me ten Shillings to lift a large tank up on top of a high building.

Sometimes there were Engines to lift out of the Aircraft for servicing (B50's) the crews had brought them in from the USA, the crews in turn had to be taken to Downham Market to catch the train for London, most of them were loaded up with their Civilian clothes all on hangers covered with see through covers, the like we never seen before. They complained about the size of the road; called out Driver! stop, when another vehicle was coming the other way, they were not quite so cocky by the time they got to the Railway station.

I was sent off to RAF Weeton again this time to learn all about Snow Ploughs. One enormous brute American called a Bross. It could clear a path Eight-foot-wide and work in up ten to fifteen-foot-deep Snow Drift, the other a Canadian called a Snow Go, this also had a blower and a loading hood. Was able to work in conjunction with a vehicle alongside loading the Snow and taking it away.

At Marham we had two sets of these ploughs and two different size Blade ploughs. And was quite well prepared to keep the Airfield open at all times.

During my stay we never had the chance to use them in Anger. I was getting away home at weekends quite often , I had an old postman cycle and made good time getting home even though it had only one gear. In the snow it took a little longer, sometimes I would stop at Newton George and have a half of beer and some crisps, more than often not; just keep going.

My goodness what would the youth of today say to be told get on your Bike.

While I was at Marham Treasa and I were Married at Coppull in Lancashire we had room's in Pentney. I was allowed to live off camp and cycle in each day.

Life in the RAF was now getting hum drum my six years was just about up, and I was quite pleased when the orderly room sent for me to hand in all my equipment and report to the Demobilization centre.

They took everything. I got on the train at Narborough with what I stood up in. I had to hand in even my forage cap and my Coat luckily; I had been able to Win the old overcoat I had exchanged after five years for a new one.

I forget the name of the Demob Station lots of us all with the same objective in mind filed onto this camp. It must have been the day for it, we were Given a large cardboard box a piece of string a Trilby hat shoes a Suite that included a waist coat and a mackintosh.

I arrived home with two weeks' pay and ration allowance about ten pounds. Now to find a job of Employment no work no pay in those days. If you could prove your entitlement one may be able to get a few shillings unemployment pays. So much for Service to King and Country . Teresa and I move into the same Cottage at Craymere we lived in as boys to start a New Life. And here I must end my tail Because the rest is all another STORY.

THE TRILBY HAT.
It seemed all so strange, people aimlessly wandering about; but obvious in knowing where they were going. I was standing on the platform at London Liverpool street station. All those years with the Blue Uniform, now the only one to be seen. I had just come from the Demobilisation centre, a lost soul slightly damp from a passing shower, they had taken everything but what I stood up in, at RAF Marham, my last engagement. Even my Cap.

Clutching a large brown cardboard box, containing, one dark suit with pin stripe, one pair of shoes, one brown Mackintosh, that would have been better out of the box, and over my shoulders, in the other hand, a large brown paper bag containing one Trilby hat, that was at any moment, to fall through the hole that was getting larger, in the bottom of this very wet bag.

Feeling conspicuously not one of the crowd, I donned the hat. What any Red Cap, "Service Police" would make of my attire at this moment, leaves little to the imagination.

I move towards the side of the platform, there were some small shops, and I would be less conspicuous.

A flight of steps down to a hair dressing Salon looked inviting, and a hair cut would pass the time until my train and make me a little presentable. Hardly had I put one foot on the first step, a little man in a mole skin, highly decorated waistcoat, came up the lower steps as though he was propelled by some invisible force. What can we do for young Sir? I being the only one in the vicinity said. "I would like a haircut please", finding difficulty in getting my words out, as I was dragged more than led, and he; wrestling the cardboard box from my grasp.

From the gloom of this lavishly decorated parlour another of the same specious came forward with much demur, possibly confused with my appearance, though dismissing his thoughts about me, but thinking of the reward,

Unbeknown to me, otherwise, I would never have gone near those steps. Leading me by the elbow to the chair, "What dose young Sir require", said he, relating some dozens of treatments he had for my desire. "A Hair cut please", I said, the Trilby hat was whisked off, a snip here, and a clip there, a squirt from a bottle of scent of some description, then the brushing of my shoulders as he guided me to the desk, where I was presented with a bill for ten shillings.

My total wealth was Two Pounds ten shillings. To the exit I was left to my own devices. Shakily I made the top of the steps, lucky to have been robed for only the ten shillings.

I had never paid more than sixpence before for a hair cut in my life, and the closest ever to the treatment received was. At the back of the billets at Marham, up some rickety steps, the words "Sit", as a red face puffing away at a cigarette, dropping ash down my shirt front, proceeded to push a pair of clippers up the back of my head, leaving me practically bald.

I made my way to the train for Norwich. Finding an empty seat, I settled down to the journey. I would liked to have gone to the Restaurant car for a cup of tea, but since my last encounter with the Highway men, I decided against it.

I arrived at Norwich Thorpe Station, only to be told the train from City Station may have left thought it did not always leave on time. Taking a chance, I ran most of the way, and arrived as the train was about to leave. Hardly shutting the door as the train moved off, my luck had changed. Hopefully it would stay so.

It was quite a nostalgic occasion, running into Melton Constable, the so familiar East box, the Coal plant, and Loco on the left of the train, the Shed and Turntable overlooked by the lord Haistings waiting room.

Stepping out of the coach on to the platform many familiar faces, Ration's Athoe plodding down the platform, his feet taking the usual east to west attitude.

Sarah Adams and her sister in the refreshment room. Father met me with the Austin Seven, 1927 Vintage that he bought from a chap at Thornage Bakehouse, for £12 during the war.

At home I picked up my Cycle, that I bought new while I was at Marham, in my last year, for £12/10.£2 down and 2/6 a week until paid for. I road with the cardboard box tied to the rear, and on my head. The Trilby hat .

On my last weekend leave, before my Demobilisation from the RAF, I had been able to rent the cottage at Craymere Beck. The same cottage that I lived in as a child, Hurdles Colman, the Steward for Mrs Chapman, Who Farmed at Thurning and Owned the cottages. It was his daughter that Married Binny Stimpson, our families being linked, certainly gave me some advantage. Though he did say, "the rent would be more than before". Two shilling and sixpence a week, one pound a month.

Teresa and my Mother would have been busy making the old cottage habitable. My last two weeks was spent at the RAF camp at Marham, while Teresa came over to Briston with our belongings, that we had accumulated during our stay in rented accommodation at Pentny, a small village nea close to RAF Marham.

It was getting dark by the time I crossed over the foot bridge at Creymere Beck, and made my way into the yard, to the back of the cottages, and the back door of the cottage. Most of the

row was in darkness having not lighted their lamps, though I doubt the lighting had not changed very little, from the days we lived in the row as children. The large step was there that Father built, but void of the porch he had erected, the little window in the back place gleamed with pearl light, and before I opened the door, I knew it was the lamp we had as children, in the same house, the one with the round burner, and pearl mantle.

Not only had I come home, the lamp had also.

At Briston they were now enjoying the luxury of the Electricity and would have no further need of it.

I opened the door, Teresa sat by a most welcoming fire in the grate of the old muck dropper. That is what Mother called that fire place, its grate was high, giving better use of the heat from the fire to the two small hobs either side, for pots and pans or the kettle. Each time it required raking out, the ashes falling to the space below, always made a mess of the hearth, Mother being very house proud would express her dislike in no uncertain terms.

Enjoying the pleasures of that first cup of tea in our new home, we discussed our immediate needs.

I had two pounds in my pocket, and hopefully next week's post, would bring the ration coupons, ration allowance and pay for my two weeks leave entitlement. Giving us the sum total of Twelve pounds. There was still two pounds a month to pay Dennis of Norwich for the furniture we had purchased previously.

We would require more Items for the house, though Mother had given Teresa quite allot of things for the house. Work must be the first priority.

In those days no work no pay, and if the rent was not paid, one may soon be out of house and home. The wage I may hope to earn, I was prepared to take anything. Though I was a qualified Motor Engineer, service qualifications did not seem to hold good for most Employers in civilian life. The average wage was about four pounds ten shillings to five pounds, for a forty-eight-hour week. We decided to call it a day and see what tomorrow may bring, lighted the candle turned out the light and went to bed.

By the light of day looking around the old place, even the wall paper in places, was as I remembered it, though the living room had been freshly decorated with a floral patterned

paper, and it still had the smell of home-made wallpaper paste, flour and water paste, and that unmistakable smell of rising damp.

We were just into the Month of June, the cold of the past winter having made its presence within the walls, I could feel the old house was glad to be lived in again.

I put the little Iron Kettle on to one of the hobs by the fire that was now burning brightly, full it contained two pints of water, freshly drawn from the well in the yard, the water jug still ringing as it touched the side of the pail, by the undulation of the water. The Kettle soon boiled for the tea, and some over for my wash, tempered by more soft water from the water tub by the back door.

The sink Father had built up on bricks was still serviceable, a typical large glazed stone sink, with a pail below to catch the water. One must take care not to let it over fill on to the floor, something Teresa will find some getting used to, having never lived in the country, and experienced our primitive ways, myself, I had no difficulty with living in the old house again, being the way's I had grown up with. It was still the most up to date house in the row. None of the others had a sink, and all the washing was done on the kitchen table, and the wash boiler in the corner of the Kitchen. Rinsing might Find for Teresa a little frustration on wash days, one sink full of water come to quite a few pails of dirty water, to be carefully drained out, and taken outside to be thrown onto the grass patch in the yard.

The clothes for drying had to be taken over the road into the appropriately named, drying ground, where each cottage, had its own two posts supporting the line.

In the centre of this quite large piece of ground, a very large Walnut tree, still shading where Fathers Goats were tethered many years since.

The toilet was still over the yard, and still contained the small box Father had made, and fixed to the wall, containing squares of paper cut from a local newspaper, very often the cause of passing humour, when A particular publication was mentioned, With. That is a fine paper to wipe your Bum on, also in the box, still the remains of a partly burnt out candle. Many is the time as lads we were severely reprimanded, for setting fire to the excess paper acuminated in the pail.

Countless times, Father had to carry this large pail all the way up to the garden, on the Burnt House road, dig a hole and bury the contents, now I am to have that pleasure.

The Garden will take much of my spare time, two large plots, and we have great hopes of good crops to supplement my wage.

Our first morning in the cottage, I wash in the sink, a bar of Sunlite soap, costing Three and a half pence, will suffice for Bathing, the tin bath, it hangs by the back door, washing the clothes and for our own daily toilet.

Bathing will as ever, be a Friday night before the fire, in the tin bath

Now before I seek my new employer this coming Monday, it is a golden opportunity to get as much of the gardens into shape, for the coming season, collect any fire wood that I can find, in and around the garden, and the nearby Coppice.

Later to become a source supply of protein supplementing our larder.

My limbs had not had the experience of heavy toil since my days working on the Railway.

The garden, as the cottage, had been neglected for many years. By the gate a Mountain, born of innumerable weeds over the past years, now composted with the exception of the outer layer, a good source of free food for this neglected soil.

I toil on, advised from time to time as to what I should or should not be doing, all with good intent, though at the time, I was a little annoyed with the attention I was encouraging.

By double digging, I was able to get most of the grass out of sight, hopefully to decay below ground, and most of the mountain of composted weeds strewn over the prepared plot .

In the other garden, I erected some posts for the Chicken Run. Mother had advised me, she intended to buy Teresa some Chickens as a house warming present. The Eggs would be very welcome.

The toils over the last two days, as the saying is, took the wrinkles out of my back.

After a good night's sleep, and a hearty breakfast, we walked up to the gardens to admire the last two days labours.

Sunday had always been a day of rest in my Family. I saw no reason for changing things now, and enjoyed the pleasures of each other's company, walking around the lanes searching for the wild flowers, that had been so commonplace in my youth. Not forgetting the birds' nests, A water hen (Moor Hen), in Mr Brownsell's Pump Pit, (Pond), contained a full clutch of cream

Eggs spotted with brown. At one time I would have had in my pocket, a dessert spoon to tie on a Hazel stick, enabling the Eggs to be taken.

We return home to a small fire in the grate, it is still cool in the evenings. Over tea I reflect how some of the families and houses had changed. The house by the Beck had completely gone, only the small barn survives on that plot of land, it had at one time been, the Blacksmith shop. As children we played there. It was there, William Hannent cut his face badly, a potato marker fell from the wall, striking him in the cheek, leaving a gash needing fourteen stitches.

He rested in our house four hours, until the Doctor came to stitch him up, the charge was sixpence, I do not remember who paid. The large farmhouse was now divided into two families. Mr and Mrs Partridge still lived in the first house in the row, ourselves in the next. Mrs Smith still living next door. The rest of the row of three cottages. People I had not become acquainted with yet. The Top house as it was always referred to, quite a large house, the house we moved into as children, the first time we came to Craymere Beck. Had now completely gone, but the signs of the old foundation still there, if one knew where to look.

Monday morning, I make my way to Manor Farm. we walked that way yesterday, but today I ride my cycle. I had been well informed that R.G.Carter were proposing to build a large barn, for Manor farm, I had great hopes there may be work for me.

I a qualified motor Engineer. But whatever paid as a wage will have to do, no work no pay, and if you do not pay your rent out you go. That is how it was in those days. And as I was later to find out. Service Qualification's did not seem to be accepted in civilian life with much regard.

At the farm, signs of some activity having been started, but at the moment no sign of life. Only just seven thirty. I take up a position enabling me to see most of the site. If and when any workmen arrive. Just after eight the Runner arrives, he is the man who keeps an eye on all the work in hand, seeing that the progresses is satisfactory. I explain my position, and much to my delight, I am told to wait for Mr George Walla, and tell him I may work with him digging the footings for the new Barn.

The wage would be just over Four pounds, for a forty-eight-hour week, they worked on a stamp card system, enabling the workman to draw his Holiday entitlement from any employer. Having paid weekly for stamps, towards the Holidays wherever entitled. This reducing the wage a few shillings.

George was a grand chap, he lived at Aylsham; alone with his aged Father, looking after him and working to keep them booth in house and home. His Father's Pension was Ten Shillings a week, George needed to take Saturday mornings off to see to the household chores, cooking and cleaning. He told me this, as I would have to carry on alone on Saturdays. The first three days completed the main part of our work for the moment on the barn site.

The runner directed us to the Dairy Farm site at Melton Constable. There we were to dig some long drains from the Stables out into a nearby field. Friday night leaving off time, George reminded me he would not be there Saturday, but to carry on following the markers. Saturday started well the digging soft, by eleven O'clock, I had dug as much as we had the day before. I decided to have a sip of tea from my bottle of cold tea in the haversack, and a snack to eat, the runner arrives, seeing me sitting on the side of the trench, he enquired as to what, I thought I was doing.

I explain my position. His reply was you must not stop, if you want a drink outside the times stated, you must work and drink. He Quotes. "Just keep drawing", If R.G.Carter see you sitting there."I will get the sack, so he sacked me instead. Saying I will be back by Twelve with your cards, and money.

It was not until just after Twelve before he returned. Seeing George sometime later he said, "I expect, that was just what they were looking for having got the outstanding work done".

Tea time that Saturday, was to say the least depressing for us. The Ten-pound leave and Ration allowance had arrived during the week, most of which was spoken for, Teresa had the promise of a cleaning job at the Duck farm in Briston, Quite a walk each day for just a few hours, and a wage of about Fifteen Shillings a week.

Just a week into our new life, one job found and lost, in just so many days. Had I made the correct move? Should I have looked near to the Industrious North. Teresa would have been near her folks.

It was with foreboding steps I walked down to the Beck that Evening.

The Air was cool, the rippling of the water as it trickled through the pipes under the road, sounded louder than ever, I could even here the Steam Engines moving about the Locomotive depot, at Melton Constable. A sure sign of Rain, When the sound carries so well.

I decided that I will try the Locomotive department next week. In the mean time I hope to get the garden finished, taking my mind off what seem a hopeless situation.

Father came down over the weekend, he brought Teresa a Meat Safe, a large box on four legs the sides and door lined with a perforated zinc material to keep the food cool and protected from any marauding blue Bottles. Fridges were unheard of as of yet, Father had made a professional job, and it looked very nice in the kitchen.

My father had been trained as a Carpenter, at the Railway works at Melton Constable, in the Carriage and Waggon shops, during the M&GN days. He served his Apprenticeship by 1921.

At that moment in time, there were no vacancy allocation, and though a skilled man, had to look for work elsewhere.

However now in 1952 he is back in his old shop carrying out his trade, repairing Waggons, and A Union Convener, but that belongs to another story.

The Monday morning I visit the Loco department at Melton Constable, there was no point in getting there to early, the Loco Foreman did not arrive until eight thirty, My luck was out the relief Foreman was standing in for him, and said, "He thought there may be something", but at the moment there was nothing he could do, Come back in a few weeks, I was told.

Disappointed, I made my way back up on to the road overlooking the loco.

I decided I must go to the Labour exchange in Holt, only to be told there was nothing at the moment, and that if I was still unemployed in one week's time, I may apply for unemployment benefit. If my National Insurance was up to date, I would be entitled to Thirty shillings.

I road back from Holt, by the Gravel Quarry at Edgefield. Curious of what the work entailed I called into the Quarry. The Foreman a little man, and very friendly gave me a brief description of how the sand and shingle was separated, and what it was used for. In fact, he remarked, "We are looking for a driver for the loader". I had been on a Coles Crane course in the RAF, so a simple loader would be no problem. The other driver was away unwell, and there was a possibility he would not return, I may start the next day. But first I must go back to the labour exchange and notify them. Back at the Labour exchange, I am told they did not know there was work at the quarry, it is our place to find work for you. "Take this card back to the quarry to be signed, saying that they require a driver".

Back at the Quarry. The Foreman was to say, the least Bemused, I replied. That I thought I had left all this Bull shit behind in the RAF.

Finally, I returned to Craymere Beck and Home, to relate this unbelievable story to Treasa, over our Megree tea. And the good fortune of starting a new job in the morning at Seven AM.

At the Quarry the power plant for the loader was, a Fordson Tractor, needing all the skill and strength one could muster to get the blessed thing started, let alone move the sloppy unstable controls.

At the face of the quarry, my job was to fill a dumper, that was then driven by another driver, to the grid, through which the load passed on its way to the washer and grader.

We were allowed four short breaks for coffee, and a bite to eat. Mid-morning, Mid-day, Mid Afternoon, and Tea time at Five O!clock. These breaks were of the duration of about ten minutes. During this time the plant must not stop. The loader driver loads the dumper, and takes it to the grid, also keep the Grid clear, and the reverse procedure for the dumper driver, our day finish at seven thirty quite a long day.

Friday pay day. Excited I cannot wait to get home to tell Teresa, a pay packet of nine pounds, seems we had struck gold. The work was hard the hours long and the Equipment falling to pieces, countless times I complained, until I was told I may take the loader to Saxthorpe garage and get it welded, though it did not last long.

The third week, part of the quarry face was falling down, I was in direct line of the oncoming sand and shingle, I slammed the reversing lever hard over, and it broke off, In the nick of time I had thrown myself out of the cab, looking back to see the sand and shingle engulfing most of the loader. It was dug out and in no uncertain terms, I quoted the Foreman all the safety regulations that had been drummed into me in the RAF.

Friday pay day again, I was informed that I was no longer required, the other man was well enough to return. However, I think they just employed another driver who would except conditions as they were.

I am not having much luck, hardly demobbed one month and lost two jobs. Where is this country fit for Heroes to come home to? That is what they keep telling us.

It rained and was cold the next day, I had hoped to get the remaining potatoes planted in the garden, I passed part of the day sawing fire wood that

I had gathered the last weekend, over the yard in our coal shed, at the moment we had not been able to afford such luxuries.

Dick Barwick was using the meadow at the back of the cottages, and the barn, the farm not being in use now since the Emersons gave up farming, Dick's Cows were in the in the barn for milking, Teresa had been in the habit of getting our milk straight from the cows, as he milked them. I said I would fetch the milk, I had known Dick for many years, and worked on his small holding after School, and at weekends.

I related the past weeks experience's, he must have taken pity on me saying, "No charge for the milk".

Sitting by the fire in the lamp light, discussing the past events, the rain pounding outside Warmed I think, our spirits, deciding to look on the bright side, hoping next week will bring more enlightenment.

Next time I went up to Briston, I took the cardboard box, called into see Mr Reynolds, he had the cycle store, and petrol pumps. Again, I related the past few weeks, also with Teresa walking to Briston to her cleaning job, a cycle would be very helpful for her, I was offered a nice new cycle.

I had intended a second hand one. I have but three pounds, my wage at the Quarry had been good, but apprehensively, I opened the cardboard box, would he care to buy a New Demob suite, I will never afford to go out in it, and a Trilby Hat. He offered me five pounds for the suite, as a down payment on the cycle, the remaining to be paid off weekly.

It Must have been the first Sunday in July 1952. One of the Neighbours gave us a Rabbit, Teresa said "how do we pluck it". The only rabbit she had seen before was in Chorley, in the butchers Shop, a feast fit for a King. I soon had the skin off, and dismembered the fore, rear, back. and basket.

All laid out in the large enamel dish mother had given us, a little onion and water, and into the oil Oven that, Mother had kindly given us.

I am afraid without those kind gifts from Mother, and others, life at the moment would be, to say the least rather austere.

The oven with our Sunday Dinner we were using, was the large Range, again another gift from Mother. This she had taken in part exchange, for a Spring-cleaning Job for Mrs Andrews. They Farmed at Hall farm Thurning, Mother was often required by Mrs Andrews to do many little sewing jobs for them, when we were young. And very glad she was to earn those few shillings, the Farther could hope to earn then was three pounds a week, and sometimes less.

The Range Had three oil burners, one was surmounted by the Oven, though it may be placed over any of the three burners. However, over the far burner, it left the two other burners conveniently placed, to take two saucepans for the vegetables. The fuel supplied the burners from a Gallon glass bottle, mounted upside down in its container, at the far end of the range. The heat may be adjusted by increasing the height of the wick.

A swede had been borrowed from the large heap. Dick Barwick had by the barn for his cows, with the potatoes and cabbage, again from Mother, this Sunday was going to be one to remember, in our first home, Tea had already been Provided for. I had been up the stream passing through Craymere, it by the way is the beginning of the River Bure. Up by Holmes Wood the water cress lay thick as grass in the water, Mother use to take us that far up for water cress. Not that it was any better than that by the Beck road crossing. I think, like I, the walk she found most pleasurable.

Monday, With Hope, and Despair, a mixture of emotions. I cycled through Briston on to the Melton Constable road, up the hill and onto the Bridge leading down to the station platform. My expectations were very low at this moment, as I dismounted from my cycle.

Walking a few yards to the start of the criss cross palings, noticeably a M&GN design.

I am to believe the brain child of one Mr Marriot, chief Designer during the early days of the M&GN Railway. To stop little boys from climbing the railings. Something a lad was bound to due attracted by the Locomotives.

I was in good time for my interview. Resting by the railings taking in all the surroundings. A little further along, the Cycle shed, placed conveniently by the steps leading down to the works, just beyond the Loco, I may leave my cycle there. Directly before me the large Turn table, at this very moment, a crew had just moved an Engine on to its platform, in the process of turning it round to face the other way. From the Chimney the purr of the Blower brightening up the fire, causing a heat shimmer to the distant view, beyond its shape. A plume of white steam issuing from the safety valves, indicating at any moment they would lift off there seat's, to a blasting roar, by the step's up to the Cab, the overflow pipes from the Injectors, dribbling water, surmounted by a small wavering mist of steam, as the boiler is being filled. Someone calls "Right Ho". A loud putt, as the Regulator is opened causing the Snifter valves to operate, the Engine moving slowly off the table, Bump, Bump, Bump, the wheels striking the permanent rail, coming off the table rail.

Steam that was issuing from the Cylinder taps, cease as the taps are closed.

To the right, the Loco shed. A figure holding a paraffin torch, dribbling its lighted paraffin to the floor, obviously the boiler washer, taking a breath of fresh air from his toils, of washing out a boiler.

In front of the shed, an early shift Engine having just returned to the Loco, being attended to. The Fire ash scattering to the floor from the cab, and through the uprights. Further on ash and coal burning on the ground awaiting the ash man's attention to clear it away.

Directly in front of me, about to be passed by the Engine now leaving the table. The Engine men's mess room and stores. And beyond, the water tanks and the Coal stage.

The crane for loading the Engines from the Coal stage, clearly visible above the shelter canopy.

To my left. The Lord Hastings waiting room, and the Platform, much activity at W.H. Smiths Book stall, situated just by the Refreshment rooms. I expect Sarah and Jenny Adams, are as busy as ever brewing up for the Leicester passengers.

Time to make my way over to the Foreman's office. Knocking on the door I am greeted with come in Mr Jackson. For a moment I was taken aback, The Foreman said. "My relief informed me of your previous visit, I am sorry I was away". My plight must have travelled beyond me.

You can start on the shed as Ash man, and with your previous experience as Fireman, you will be available for steam raising or other duties I trust. I was over whelmed, as I replied I would be delighted to take up any position offered. He gave me a Rail Ticket to Norwich, and a letter for the Medical officer at Norwich Thorpe. Saying, "If you satisfy the Medical officer you can start Tuesday and count Monday as part of your first week".

Returning home, I could hardly wait to tell Teresa the good news and passed that time up in the garden. The potatoes I had planted, had just shown through here and there, the grass was well in advance of the potatoes, my admirer's leaning over the gate, in particular Mr Smith from next door. "You won't git no spuds in all that lot. "They will git smothered in grass. "We shall see," I replied, and continued to clear away the weeds and grass from where I could see a trace of potato growth.

It was time to go back to the house, Teresa now having the cycle will be home in good time, she was delighted with my news.

In the morning, I decided to cycle to Hindolveston Station, it was slightly nearer than Melton Constable Station. By the time I got to the old tin barn at the junction leading to the gate House, I realised I was not going to catch that train. There was nothing for it but to Cycle to Foulsham, and through on to the Norwich main road.

Having cycled from Briston to Feltwell, Briston to Marham, many times on week end pass, in all kinds of weather, even once on a borrowed old single gear Postman's cycle. This would be a Doodle.

I also had the advantage of not having to walk from City Railway Station, I could cycle down to Norwich Thorpe and the Medical centre. I had been there before for my Medical, when I was to be expected as a Cleaner those years previous.

The room was full of men awaiting to see the Doctor, though thankfully, I did not have to wait long. I was more concerned for the safety of my cycle than of passing the medical.

This I expressed to the Doctor on entering his surgery. Sounding my chest, he said. "If you have cycled all the way from Briston there can't be much wrong with you and gave me the necessary letter to take back to the Loco Foreman.

I was to start work at the Loco the next day, Clearing up Ashes, a labouring job, the wage about Four to five pounds a week. I cycled to my parents' house, Hunted through the sheds for my old metal food box, the one I had as a fireman. I had paid ten shillings for it, by weekly instalments to Mr Daulton the NUR Secretary. They were made by a firm of Ironmongers in Grimsby, it had my name on the brass plate. Now I can go back to the Loco in Style.

In the meantime, Treasa had just received a letter from her Mother, we understood she had moved into a new home, her Husband had died some years previous. There was some trouble, the nature of what we had no inclination. Teresa wanted to go up to Lancashire, I suggested she wait a few days, because now as an employee of the Railway, I could get a privilege ticket, saving a considerable amount of money, that at this moment in time we were in need of.

Another day another start. I tie my old food box onto the cycle and make the journey to the Loco at Melton Constable. I leave my cycle by the old, Lord Hastings waiting room. At the moment I had no Idea where I may leave it. There was a well-trodden path by the Turntable leading to the Engine Mans mess room, and the Signing on.

Mr Grint was still in charge of the stores, assisted by Tom Nobes. A small kindly man with a large Wart on his face. I remembered them well from my cleaning days. Tom was the unofficial Medical Officer, one of the Drivers thought it great fun to have all new boys wait, the pleasure of Mr Nobes, the Loco Medical. Having them wait in the signing on,

telling them all sorts of weird Operations they would have to perform, during this fictitious Medical, until terror obvious in the face of the victim, indicated time to tell the lad it is all a joke.

I am expected, given a work ticket to fill in and told to go to the rear of the stores where I may sign for one LNER Shovel. The rest I was familiar with, having worked on Ashes many times as a cleaner. It was an eight-hour shift, with a half hour out for meal break. First, I had to shovel out of the two pits in front of the shed, ashes that had been deposited there since yesterday. The pits about four-foot-deep the ashes wet and heavy, to be thrown on to the side of the pits. Usually a low sided wagon placed by the shed, Engine Crew, just clear of the pits themselves. Having cleared the pits, a pinch bar was needed, usually to be found on the floor just inside the Engine shed. A long bar about five-foot-long with the end shaped to a wedge. Surprisingly with the wedge well under the flange of the waggon wheel and lean down on the bar, the waggon could be moved with relative ease.

The hard work was to come, throwing the wet ash up over the side of the waggon, this part over it was acceptable to go into the Mess room for a brew up, and little snack. I had with me my Billy can, that had been with me since I was at Colwick Loco.

No respectable Crew were without a Billy at Colwick.

Next task was to go around the Loco clearing up any ash that had been deposited about the track. In addition, the ash man was available for any other tasks that may require a labour. Many of the mundane tasks were given to any Cleaners that may be on the Shed, and they, only too glad to get them. This gave them a shorter day, a labouring job called for a half hour meal break.

Sometimes a waggon load of sand needed to be loaded into the Sand hopper, for drying and sifting.

This was for use in the Engine sand boxes to stop the wheels from slipping on the rails, some Engines had steam sands enabling the sand to be blown on to the rail, others were mechanical. A rod to the sand box gave the fireman control over the amount of sand he may let fall on to the rail. Should this sand not be dry and sieved, there may be obvious problems.

Often, we placed potatoes in the sand to cook, the heat from the fire maintained below the sand hopper, gave a nice slow cooking time to the potatoes.

These are briefly the tasks; I shall be doing for the time being. During the week I made friends with a chap working on the shed, I think he was in the Boiler smith shop. During a discussion about relieving the local Squire, of some of his Game to supplement the meagre wage, he suggested a compression rifle he had for sale. he brought it to work, and demonstrated its capability's, he fired a number three ball through a thick door, I was impressed.

The stock needed charging with air, using a pump, the ammunition was made from heated lead, poured into a tool provided. I could not afford the weapon, though my brother was at the time very interested. Father and my Brother, now working over in the Carriage and waggon shops, I could slip away from time to time and see them.

My labours followed this routine for some time, the Odd diversion to cleaning the Foreman's office, off-loading supplies for the firelighter store, and general dogs' body.

Teresa had gone up to Chorley to see her mother. I had applied for a privilege ticket. This was a great help with the Fare. Without that we she would have had to wait a few weeks, until funds were available. The potatoes in conflict with the grass, most of my spare time spent keeping the weeds down, avoiding the usual audience, that seem to appear from nowhere. Clicking their tongue's saying. "He won't git any spuds there".

Teresa returns with an addition to our family, a little Girl barely three years old, her mother not able to look after her. Teresa always a sucker for a hard luck story, had taken Linda. "That was the child's name", for a while until her Mother was able to look after her again. It was going to be difficult making ends meet, there was no help from the State, in those days, it all had to be provided from what I could earn. We had many commitments just starting out a family life. Little did I realise it would take another ten years, and another addition before Mother was wanting her offspring returned.

Linda had problems, continual Bed wetting, for this she got reprimanded Severely, on more than one occasion, and with Teresa now restricted in how often she was able to get to her work, there was friction on more than one occasion. However, life settled down, my work varying.

I have been notified I am to relive one of the coal men, at the Engine Coal plant, this one of the job's, unpopular with most. Two shifts, eight until Four and Four until Twelve, or whenever the last Engine is in and Coal'd.

I was to relieve Bill Adams, Joe Horne to be my mate, a good worker. I had worked with him many years before. A week of Eight until Four, every morning all the tubs were empty, the ruling was to fill them all before leaving off, this seldom happened. To get those tubs filled before an Engine came to take one or more was quite an effort, the Aim was to get all tubs full, each one contained Half a Ton, and down to the coalman's rest room for a cup of tea. By the time one had achieved that, a cup of tea was very welcome.

Next week the late shift. I had in mind to do something in the quest, regarding Meat for our larder another mouth to feed, no Benefit Department to run to in those days.

My brother had acquired that Rifle, the air chamber was not holding the Air, on inspection, the valve made of wood, had seen the best of its days. I was confident in being able to make a new one, if I could find something to turn a piece of wood to pattern.

In discussion with Joe over a cup of tea. I was on the late shift now coal stage. he said, "Have a look in the Machine shop, there are plenty of Lathes in there". During a lull, and all the tubs full, I ventured to the Machine shop, it was just by the Chair Legs, the Apparatus for lifting the Engines. At times there was a need to lift an Engine to remove bearings for metal work. In the Machine shop, in the dark, I located the main switch, and Frightened myself by starting all the shaft's running. The shaft's turning the belts to the machinery, causing enough noise to waken the dead.

Swiftly I turned all off, with the exception of the grind stone. Well I could make a start in shaping the new valve. I had noticed that the nut holding the grinding wheel on, had some threads extending beyond the shaft, and my piece of wood just screwed into the threaded portion of the nut, quite firmly.

I returned to the coal stage for a while, and at the next opportunity, returned and with the aid of a tool made from an old file, made my simple valve. Triumphant I returned to the coal stage; I think Joe was as pleased as I.

Returning home, the valve fitted, and upon charging the stock with Air, woke the whole house banging the pump on the floor. The last part of the compression needed, that kind of treatment to overcome the pressure already in the chamber.

There was no leak, the Rifle worked quite simple, the stock charged with Air, screwed to the barrel, the barrel contained a spring-loaded rod, tension to the spring by turning a Key, locked by a button that protruded on the left side of the barrel. A number three ball previously made from lead with the provided tool, rammed down the barrel, and the rifle was ready to use.

By placing the stock through the bib and brace of my overall, it left my right hand free to hold a torch, the firing button on the left enabled me to use my left hand to press the button, that released the tension on the spring, allowing the rod to strike the valve I had made. Momentarily allowing sufficient compressed air to discharge the ball. Exceedingly pleased with myself I retired for the night.

Working the late shift, I was able to get forward with the potatoes. Trying to pull some earth up to them, my watchful observer there as usual. "You got more grass up than you have muck", "you won't git nothing under there" "We shall see", I replied, Hopefully. Dick Barwick was seeing to his Cows, behind the barn I strolled over on my way back to the house. "What about the news", he said explaining something he had herd on the Radio. "We have no Radio or Papers, come to that Dick". Was my reply, can't afford them.

I keep looking around for any little job, after work or weekends. "You can cut all that old Furze down on my piece by the Gatehouse if you like for Two pounds". I agreed to get it done the rest of the week, being I was on late shift.

I had my early tea and started off for Melton Constable, and my shift on the Coal stage. The rifle wrapped in a sack; the stock well charged with Air. I took the lane up by Ridlands Barns, the Keepers house, and over the Railway line, to the Hindolveston road, and to the Works entrance, by the old water tanks.

On my way I had familiarize myself with any likely places I may find some Game on my return journey.

During the shift it started to rain, and continued all night, dashing any hope's I had of something for the Pantry, a steady drizzle I would not have minded, but wet from a hard shift, and raining cats and dogs, I was only too glad to cycle home by the road through Briston.

It was not the first time I had road home through the lanes. The driving rain making it much darker than usual, with what little light the lamp on my cycle could muster.

As I approached the opening that took the footpath, and short cut to the Village. A sensation of not being alone. This was not the first time at the same spot over the years, I was aware of a companion. Years ago, as a passed Cleaner on the Railway, at the same spot, a large black dog trotting beside me as I ride along. I even said, "Hello my man" Though the wind and the rain for some uncanny reason had stopped.

All was quiet, though, there should have been the clicking of claws on the road surface. But there were none. He slowed down and passed to the rear of my cycle, and into the opening to the footpath. Make of it what you will. Old Shuck stills roams the, High ways and by ways, all over Norfolk.

Elated as I was to have felt the presence of an old friend again. I cycled rapidly Home forgetting my quest for meat for the larder. Was I asleep, had I dropped off? Or just dead tired from my toils.

To bed, and to dwell on the present needs. I had promised to clear those Furze off the land near the gate house, for Dick Barwick.

The two pounds, I intend to use as a down payment on a Radio of some kind. It may help to ease the Tension that was now ever present in our House hold.

I am up early. A breakfast of bread and Milk, Courtesy of Dick Barwick. A cheese sandwich in my pocket, I hope to get as much done today as possible, weather permitting, the Furze had been neglected for a long time. In the past it had been the practice of burning it off.

Though I had my suspicion, it was more of a kindness to my needs for a few extra pounds, Dick made the offer. Some of the stems were over two inches thick. The hook I had was a poor representative of a Gurkha knife, each blow to the stems brought down a shower of prickles, falling, most of them, down my neck. The end of the day and time to go home, and get ready for my next shift, on the Coal Stage at Melton. The way things were going it was going to take all week to get it all cut down.

The end of my next shift, Joe had told me I may get away early, as soon as the Tubs were full, it was Eleven thirty by the time I got off the works, and on to the Hindolveston road. There was a field of Swedes by the Dairy Farm, I decided to get one, It was a clear night, I could see to cut away most of the soil and leaves, then I dropped the blessed thing, it rolled away down to the bend in the road, not wanting to show a light, I fell over it, however at least some addition to the larder.

The night being clear I had little hope of seeing anything up a tree before it saw me. My assumption true, I arrived home meat less. I had intended to go out again to the fields by the Barn, but my day cutting Furze, and a Shift on the coal stage, taking its toll. I fell asleep over my cup of tea and it was daylight again before I awoke. The rest of the week was work and more work. Attempts with the rifle on the way home was fruitless, I must get a torch that will give a beam. During the war years at Norwich City Station, the American services had a dump near the goods yard. We often searched through the waste, and many of their hand torches had been rejected, some just because the batteries were exhausted. I was sure there must still be one at home in Fathers shed. By extending the battery container, more power may be obtained. Should I be able to afford the Battery's, with an addition like that to my Armoury, I would have a better chance of a rabbit at night.

Friday night on starting my shift on the Coal Stage, the Foreman sent for me. What had I done wrong had I been reported for my attempts at poaching? Private life or not, the Railway condemned any activities that may bring disrespect, even though their employees. "How are you getting on the Forman said", Its hard graft isn't it. I replied, "I could find no fault with that statement. He smiled. Of course, you know the Footplate is out of the Question, your Seniority lie's at Colwick, there is many before you, unless they all leave at once. I could not see that happening and as things were, I was glad of a job anyway.

I would like you to start next week on days, steam raising" he said. As having been a Fireman you are the most suitable of the Labouring staff, there will be some Tube sweeping from time to time". I thanked him kindly and returned to Joe on the Coal Stage. Saying, "well you will have Billy back next week to torment you".

The Saturday morning early, I went over to the wood behind the cottages. I took the Rifle, hopefully a rabbit at least, we had but a swede and some potatoes and corned Beef, in the pantry for weekend. I had but got into the wood, it was barley light.

I saw some movement further in, it was too tall for a rabbit. A figure, a man, it was either, Billy Hall or Mr Jenkins. It was the later.

I hurriedly gathered as much loose wood I could find nearby, bunched it up around the rifle.

By the time he noticed me and came over, I had quite a good pile of wood. I said, "I hoped he did not mind me taking wood from his plantation". He said very little and moved off. Thanking my blessings, I returned home with at least something to keep us warm over the weekend.

After a bowl of bread and milk, I returned to the Furze. During the morning Dick came over, and said, "he thought I had done a good job" and gave me the two pounds.

Eagerly I went up to Briston, found the torch as I had hoped for in Fathers shed. Called at Mr Reyonlds Shop, he tried two battery's in the torch, and it worked fine.

I also acquired on hire purchase a Radio. It was a Bakelite cased radio. Long and medium wave, Called, Ocean Queen, Battery Electric.

At the time we had no electricity. My two-pound gone, I hoped Teresa would approve of the purchase. A little harmony at this time would make life tolerable. A letter from her mother, she wanted Teresa to have the other two children, Peter and Pauline, Twelve and Eleven years old respectively. I had no argument with that if she thought we could coupe. Little did I realise that they would be added to our Bill of fare. As I understood, there would be no finance accompanying the children.

As mentioned before, there were no Benefit Office to run to for assistance.

Would we eventually end up in the Workhouse? Oh! yes, there were still a few in operation. Thursford for one Example.

Saturday Night after dark, with my torch and the rifle fully charged, I walked up to the gardens and the field beyond, it had been cut for hay, sweeping the torch over the grass a rabbit appeared in the beam of light, it was quickly mine, home and skinned for the weekend meal. Remorseful at having to take such steps. Yet like many others in my situation, had very little other option.

I am still looking for this land fit for Hero's to come home to. Service men seem to be the last persons wanted as employees. I never could see the reason for that. Service Trade training was very thorough.

My first day back Steam Raising. I thought there would have been some resentment, though there seem to be plenty of Firing turns for past cleaners. As a passed cleaner, we found the firing jobs to say the least, not too plentiful.

I soon found my way around the Engines that were in steam, and those that were in for wash out and required the fires removed.

To make up a fire that was about to be shovelled out on to the ground, would provoke some strong words from the Crew having to do that job, I was quite certain off that.

Steam raising after two weeks on the Coal Stage was a doodle, just to keep a little fire in the fire box, and water in the Boiler, took a lot less effort than filling those coal tubs.

On occasions I was required to sweep a set of tubes. This a job I hated as a passed cleaner, then only a mere lad, often in the darkness, perched up on the front of an Engine over the pits,

to fall I would have certainly broken something. However, we completed the job and came back for more. Sweeping the tubes, it was required to take a very long rod with an eye at the end, filled with thick string called a Tow, and pass through each boiler tube, from the smoke box to the fire box, hopefully removing the soot and deposits from each tube. I never counted them but there must have been at least Fifty tubes perhaps more. If it was raining, the soot wet on your hands burnt, and dried out any natural oils one may have had on one's palm.

Not the best of jobs for a lad, to have worn gloves for such work, would have invited scorn from the old hands.

I was steam raising for a few weeks, with the exception of the time the coal crane, was out of order. Then any one available was put to work filling the Engine Tenders, from any point where an Engine and coal wagon, may be placed at a set of points, allowing the coal to be thrown up by hand.

A thankless task, more so when I was cleaning. Young lads, in a waggon trying to get coal up on to the Tender, especially in the dark, what little light about the Loco came from a fluttering Gas jet, aided by the usual paraffin torch, that having been tilted to give more light from excess paraffin, running on to the wick, made black choking smoke, making life more difficult. More than often in those situations Nature decided a good rainstorm would help things. There were oils skins provided at the coal stage, though the heat in that clothing was worse than getting wet. Thankfully hand coaling was not to regular.

The other two children arrived. Not bad children rely, though the lad had no experience of the country ways, a few things the local people just left about as was the practice, found their way to our door.

Though I will say some large sheets of tin were brought home, to help make a porch over the back door. I had mentioned the fact that, I would build a porch having the material, but at the moment could not afford it. Also, a cycle. A very dilapidated cycle, but as I explained, most of things people had around the village were in some state of disrepair. It did not mean no one wanted them.

They were not bad children, just not use to our ways. The radio was soon without battery's, we had only used it for the news, and on Sunday afternoon, they wanted it on all the time, and could not understand, we had not the money to buy more batteries. My wage under Five pound a week, the commitments needing paying each week, left little for trivialities.

Teresa finding it difficult to keep up her little job, there seemed was no formulae for harmony, in the household.

It was getting into Autumn. I took the lad Chest-nutting in the woods by the stream, what should have been an interesting outing, seemed to terrify the lad. Surrounded by houses and people all his life. I suppose I should have expected no more.

I decided a day at the Sea side. The weather was still quite nice, I applied for privilege tickets for the four of us, Linda was under five so required none. Our day out at the sea side was to Sheringham, they had nice day on the sands, we had taken our own food to save on the expense of buying anything. I think our outlay for the day was three, three penny Ice cream's, and three sixpenny sticks of Rock to bring home. At least they enjoyed the day out. Harmony reigns supreme for a while anyway.

About the middle of the next week back at work, again the foreman sends for me. I had little apprehension this time, I was doing my work well, perhaps promotion. That was a foregone conclusion.

The Foreman, in a stern mood. "I have a complaint from the Station Master, he understands you acquired privilege tickets for two children". "Yes, that is true," I replied, "also one for my wife and myself". But he said, "The Station master said they are not your Children". Again, I replied, "that is true, but they are in my care, at my expense". I explained the situation, the foreman said he hoped he could amend the accusation, though he expects, I should have to pay the excess, on the children's Fare.

And that was the case. I was lucky not to have lost my job. The Station Master by the way was a relative. It is said you can choose your friends, but not your relations. That is true, as I can Vouch for That.

Having got over the despondent feeling of the last few days. I turned my attention to the potatoes, they were having a struggle to maintain their heads above the grass, though managing with plenty of top. He was there again, like Magic my chief audience leaning on the gate. All top and no bottom.

Those words repeatedly. I decided with apprehension to lift a root of the potatoes, the fork came out with a potato as big as your foot, stuck to one of the tines, I casually said. "That always seem to happen doesn't it? you always prick the big ones". Mr Smith's Jaw dropped, about three inches, as I lifted the rest of that root, containing three more potatoes as large as the first, accompanied by more the size of hen's eggs. I decided to take them all up when, I had the time available, and Make a Hod in the other garden with straw. Some call it a Hale but Father always said it was a Hod. A shallow scrape is made on the soil, covered with straw as the potatoes are placed on the straw, the sides are covered with more straw, up to a Cone shaped top, the whole then covered with soil, leaving a tuft of straw out of the top for ventilation. This was my intention.

Back to work Steam Raising. In addition, I was to help the Boiler Smith. Now I can enter the Holy of Holy's. There Hidey Hole.

As cleaners we always wondered what it was like in there, a room on the end of the shed, next to the Fitting Shop, about ten feet by six feet. I announce my presence, the door opens but a few inches, showing the gloomy interior, a bloodshot Eye twinkled, inviting me in. Up on the wall a gas jet fluttered, blackening the wall even more so, if that was possible. Mr Miller Snigger, lounging at the far end on a long locker, that I assumed was also used to sleep on, during the night shift, when needed.

Hello young Peter", he said. How are you? He then started reminiscing, remembering the years gone by, when he was Principle Cornet, in the Briston Silver band, with My father, and Uncle David. He said, "his mate was leaving soon, and had asked for me to take his place for the time being", "as Boiler Smith's mate". I had no objection to that. I was also to continue with Steam Raising, it was one of the Boiler Smith jobs any way.

I leave the Boiler Smith and his mate, to continue my tour of the Engines in Steam, just through the side door, and on the sand hole road, stands a Knock John.

The name given to a Class J15 0-6-0. Though, a Title shared with other J Class Engines. My Charge has been left by the shed crew, shortly after my last round of inspection. The fire was low, and the boiler water gauge indicated, a need to put the Injectors on to replenish the Boiler, I placed a small quantity of coal just under the door to keep the fire alive. The Engine was not required until the next day. After opening the valve from the Tender allowing the water to flow down to the feed pipe, and tapping lose the steam key to the Injector, the clack coming into operation, commenced to pick up the water and force it into the boiler.

Sitting in the cab pondering over my good fortune, and what, Mr Miller had said. That I would properly be required to go to Norwich Thorpe, to learn how a brick arch is built, in a fire box. Though, I would most likely have had plenty of experience with his mate doing just that, before the Trip to Norwich.

The sound of the singing Injector, as it filled the boiler, arousing Memories of my cleaning days. It was in this very same spot, I opened my first Regulator. The device allowing steam to the pistons driving the wheels, had I have been caught in the act, my Railway career would have ended abruptly, there and then. Barely sixteen years old, with no thought to the complications that it may evolve. Putting the Reversing lever to the forward position, gingerly opening the Regulator, the Engine moves forward. Resisted by the tender, whose hand brake was still on. Rapidly closing the Regulator and acting as though nothing had happened. I doubt very much that I was the first cleaner to do just that.

A noise behind and above me, aroused from my reminiscences. Someone putting their cycle away in the cycle shed, up on the Hindolveston road. The road runs along the rear of the works, and at a much higher level. From the cycle shed, one may look down and over most of the Loco, and the Station.

Between my position in the warm cab, runs another track under the Chair legs to the buffer stops at the embankment.

The Chair legs a massive crane like structure. Four massive legs spanning the Rail. Progressing upwards, converging at a platform, containing the pulley gear required, to enable the reduction to be obtained in lifting the weight of an Engine, enabling the fitters to remove the big ends from the Engine. They, then taken the short distance into the Machine shop for metalwork.

Power for lifting, came in the form of four cleaners, and two large cranks, one had to turn many times before any sign of movement, could appreciably be seen. There again work eagerly contested for, by any cleaner, with it was the, Title. Labouring, Carrying with it, the entitlement of, half an hour meal break, and a few coppers extra in the pay packet.

Moving up to the next Engine in line. A Claud Hamilton, the cab with side windows giving greater protection from the Elements. Working tender first into the rain, or Snow, was a different matter. The Claude was required again for the Tea time passenger to Norwich, had need of little attention from me.

A nice fire, the Boiler water gauge indicated, that it would stand until required, without further attention. There is no need to vacate my comfortable seat immediately. Gazing to the scrap bins by the machine shop, containing old brake blocks, and oddments of scrap, including old burnt out fire bars from the boiler smiths' shop. I expect shortly, that will be one of my jobs. The tall chimney of the Foundry having been silent since the close of the, Carriage and waggon shops. When the M&GN had the monopoly of most of the local work force, now just partly used by the Boiler smith shop, storing fire bricks, and the clay to build the brick arches. Directly before me, the rails in front of the Foreman's office, where a wood walk way crosses the rails, that converge, at numerous sets of points, setting the track to the Engine Shed, or Turn Table.

At the far end of the Loco. Conveniently placed, the Coal stage, at one side of the track, and the large water tanks the other.

At one time the large space below the tanks, housed the Boiler for pumping water, supplying not only the Loco, but railway workers house in the village. This space now the rest room for the Coal men.

Exit from the Loco, at this point controlled, by a set of points and a Semaphore, operated from the East signal box, that was situated at the far end of the Station Platform. A blast of seven whistles from an Engine, indicating to the signal man, an Engine wishes to leave the Loco.

Life at home progresses into the cold days of approaching winter. Warm clothes are needed for the family. Much of our shopping restricted to Mrs Sexton's Shop in Hall Street, there we could get our shopping on the book, and settle up at week end. The other large shop for clothing was Mr Yallop, a very large store for a village. They sold everything one may require. Drapery. Provisions. And Hardware. It was fortunate that we were able, to get most of the things we needed, also on the book. Not many people at those times had very little option.

F.W.Yallop. This was a very large store for a village, It had always been so. Before Mr Yallop It was under the Proprietor, a Mr A.H. Roe and before that, Mr Rivett. All the owners were very enterprising. The shop displayed the name and its Business taking practically the whole length above the large display windows. Warterloo House, Draper, Milliner, Outfitter, Grocery. There was not much one may not buy, and it was delivered by an errand boy.

A copy of Briston Records. Tips for the times. Mr Rivett boasts. "You can't get anything cheaper. Anywhere". And the list is endless. Sugar 1½d lb, Pure Lard 5½d lb, Tea 1/ lb. Blankets 6/9 a pair. Boots for men 4/11d, Woman 2/11d, a very colourful list, dated 1894.though I expect those people shopping in 1894 could do little more than I, in 1952. Window Shop. We obtained the clothing necessary for the immediate needs, the rest will have to take the form of Christmas presents.

Late September and the potatoes are in the hod, some of the garden cleared, and planted with cabbage plants of some description. My audience have taken kindly to me, and gifts of plants, that I find often by the Garden gate. My notoriety with lamp and Rifle is brought to the attention of one local land owner. I receive a call from the Steward. Fortunately, his daughter married one of our close relatives, he tips me off, and tells me to go somewhere other, than on their land for a while.

I find it strange; the Farmers are constantly claiming the damage the Rabbit dose to his crop yet denies the odd man his addition to the pantry.

I make friends with the man living in the old farm house, now divided and housing two families. He a little older than I. To help expand our meagre wage, he a farm worker, recently demobbed from the Army finding it difficult to make ends meet. We decided at the weekend to go to Stiffkey marshes, and gather Cockles, we were going to sell them, and make a few shillings. In my shed there was a Tandem Cycle.

Can you ride tandem, Arthur?". "Yes, if you steer" was the reply. It was a fine Saturday morning we got away in good time, so as to catch the tide going out. By midday we had gathered four bags of cockles, the bags being sand bags, two hanging over the cross bar and two behind my seat, by the time we had pushed the tandem along the field path to the road, we knew we had quite a load.

The ride home was uneventful with the exception of the run down the hill past Hindringham Church. A heard of cows decided at that moment to cross the road, it was more by luck than judgement the tandem staid upright, bouncing from cow to cow, emerging unscathed but rather shaken.

Back at Craymere Beck, the tin bath filled with water, and cockles for washing. Selling them was another thing, we even tried the Public house at opening time just up the road, at sixpence a pint we only sold two pints. Eventually what we could not eat we gave away at the local cottages. What we hadn't realise was, the regular shell fish Hawker had been round whilst we were cockle digging.

Back to the Loco, only to find the Coal plant out of action again. No Engine could get up to the Coal stage. One of the early Engines over a slight misunderstanding between Driver and fireman, regarding the signal. Resulted in the Engine passing the signal at danger and going off the line at the points. Whose purpose it was to do just that, should they be crossed at danger. The Permanent way gang tried with what means they had available, to no avail to get the Engine back on to the rail. It was now a matter of waiting for the Steam Crane to come from Norwich Thorpe, when it was available. It had to go the long way around to Cromer first. This meant all available hands including me. Hand Coaling the tenders, the only good thing to come out of it was a little overtime.

By next day all was back to normal. I am to join the boiler smith and his mate, Mr Sid lot I think it was, a very nice quiet gentleman from Hindoleveston. There was quite a long rest period before we started the day, a tube to be replaced on one engine, this I was interested to see. Luckily, I was told, the tube end in the smoke box came free enabling the tube to be screwed from the firebox end, the new one screwed in and burred off at the smoke box end. A fire bar we replace in another engine.

Later in the week I was to help Mr lock build a brick arch. There were two Arched boards, two because the firebox door was not wide enough to pass the width of an arch, required for the whole Arch to be built.

A selection of fire bricks, and some clay, that Mr lock had shown me the correct constituency needed. It was my job now to go into the Fire box and pull down what was left of the old Arch, it was not uncomfortable in the fire box, and surprisingly spacious, I crawled through the opening into the Fire box, and started knocking with my hammer, not as easy as I expected. A face at the fire hole door. "Put your back into it", "I'm doing my best said I" "No get under and push up with your back. It came down either side of me, with very little effort. After clearing the bricks away, Mr lock exchanged places with me.

I passed the two Arch boards through to him, watching as he placed them on to the raised stay heads forming an Arch. The bricks he had placed on the footplate in the order I was to pass them through. First the headers, they were shaped, that they may rest against the boiler on the lugs, and on the Arch to begin the building, the rest of the fire bricks tapered like a wedge, though only slightly. "Make sure to get the thick end to the top", he said. When the Arch was bricked from side to side, I passed in the clay, that he pushed down between the spaces in the fire bricks. At this moment the arch board, and new brick arch are as one. I pass in the slate. Just the same slate as one would find on a roof, broken into pieces about the size of the fire bricks, but not as wide.

Starting in the middle of the Arch, those pieces of slate now tapped in between each brick evenly, from centre outwards. I could see now Why, as the new brick Arch began to rise off the boards, allowing the Arch boards to be withdrawn. "You could sit on that now", he said. "It will not come down in a hurry". Finally, the remaining clay is plastered over the top the arch, smoothing off any irregularity. At the first firing, all the clay under the intense heat forms into a glass like substance, completing the operation . Protecting the Tube face from the intense heat of the fire, also diverting the fire around the box in the most efficient way.

Signs of winter coming ever nearer, I spend much of my time not at work, gathering fire wood. If I found a log or a limb from a tree, once it was on my shoulders, I done my very best to keep going until I reached the garden, where a cover previously built would keep it dry, until it was sawn into suitable size for the grate.

There is talk of a hard winter, frost and snow, the hedges thick with berry's, Hazel nuts in abundance. Plenty of Chestnuts, I am told by my ever watch full Neighbour, I could vouch for the Chestnuts. Having been over to Holm's wood, and gathered nuts from the fallen leaves, quite a quantity of good sizable nuts.

Some I stored, as I had the potatoes, covered with straw, others in a large tin, separating each nut with sand, and burying the tin in the garden.

Teresa was able to get in a few hours work, but with our ready-made family it was not easy. Just under £5 a week, and quite a few outstanding Items to pay off. Over time on occasions was a big help. But most of the time, the outgoing never, balanced the income. I was thankful for the Rifle. Though at times, I came near to more than one scrape.

There were wild Duck on a large pond, I was in close vicinity of my target, I heard Voices, I dived for the cover of a large clump of Bracken, I watched as the land owner, and her Son and their dogs walked by my hide. After they had gone out of my sight, the rifle being virtually silent. With my duck, I made haste home.

Some weeks later, heeding the well-meaning warning from the farm steward. I had been trying my luck after dark, over by Holme's Wood, and adjacent meadows.

A light in the distance seamed to move every time I moved, If I walked to the right or left, it moved with me, I ducked down, it disappeared only to reappear as I got up. Getting concerned, thinking I was being stalked by an army of Gamekeepers, not looking where I was going. I should have heard the heavy breathing, suddenly I was surrounded by a herd of Cows, some trying to get up having been laying on the grass. Luckily, I managed to extract myself from their midst unscathed. The light steadier as the Moon had risen. The added light assured me, my would-be assassins were, no more than a light over the porch at the Farm in the distance.

I would often take the rifle to work with me on the four O'clock coal stage turn, and see what I may find on the way home, sometimes I would go down the Hindolveston road as far as the dairy farm, and cut through the estate fields, over the Railway line out onto the Ridland's plantation, sometimes to Holmes wood, not always was I able to get anything, walking over fields half carrying the old cycle, half pushing then falling into ditches was not all fun.

You hear of people talk of moonlight nights and Pheasants up trees, you can forget it, no moon a clear sky, and a little rain is the kind of night for Pheasants .

I never got a Rabbit on a wet night, when I had my Rabbit or whatever, I did not go out again until we wanted more.

The variable hours were getting me down , I had my share of shift work on the railway's years ago and wanted something more steady .

The two elder children went back to Lancashire to their Mother . Linda remained with us.

Marshals Flying school of Cambridge, were moving the No 2 C.A.A.C.U from Little Snoring to Langham, and looking for ex RAF personnel, to work there.

I apply and am successful. later I will insert my Langham story.

Tereasa has another job with Smith's Newspapers from the bookstall at Melton, delivering papers by cycle to the outlying villages, quite a job of work in all weathers, on occasions I am able to help, she was certainly a glutton for hard work.

We move up to a small cottage in Briston, next to the Chequers public house. loo and behold, her Mother present us with another off spring, this time of a few weeks old Carrol.

The house is one room down, and one and a half up. Not very large for the four of us, now an old lady who was very helpful, gets turned out of her lodgings. Treasa always a soft touch takes her in. Now we are a house full. Though her help was very much appreciated. Here we had Electricity but no water, only from the well .

It must have been about 1956, a call from the local Authority, declaring we were overcrowded, Again I think, some well-wisher doing us a favour, and we are offered a Council house at Hindringham.

We move to Hindringham about 1956, not so far now to go to work at Langham. I am still riding the stink wheel. A Cycle Master, a small engine of 50cc built into a wheel, and fitted into a cycle. Kenny had one that was only 25cc.

They served us well, though often needed decoking , they ran very well on Aviation Fuel.

I needed some means of getting the family about, on occasions. There was a motor cycle combination for sale at Holt. A Mr Dawson of the cycle shop, he took me down to his allotment, there was the machine partly covered with a tarpaulin and weeds.

A New Imperial 500 cc, quite an impressive machine in its day, advanced for the year 1936, it had a springing heal, the rear wheel and frame, pivoted about the gearbox chain sprocket, supported by two large springs fixed to the main frame just under the seat, also a foot change for the gears, that proved to be faulty. I converted it into a hand change that worked very well, the gear box needed some thrust washers. I decided to make them, but first I needed a lathe.

I could not afford one, but I knew my Grand Mother had an old treadle sewing machine, fortunately I was in her favour, and she gave it to me. It was not too difficult to make up a head, I could manage without a chuck. One can always find a way to turn the work. The problem was, not enough weight in the flywheel. As soon as I tried to turn the work using the cutting tool, it rapidly slowed down. However, a small dustbin lid duly weighted with lead, and I was able to work the washers to the size I wanted.

The Engine after a Decoke was as good as new. We now had a means of a ride out. Carrol just a toddler, called it Daddy's pram. One trip was to Lancashire, Treasa had gone up by train taking Linda and Carrol for a few days with their Mother. I rode up later, not being able to lose time off work.

I remember the look on the faces of some young gentlemen, as I rode up the backs of the houses at Coppull. A large black hut, it was the local barber shop, next day the same people were by the shop with a car, half in and half out of there small garage, it was a MG. One chap came up to me, and asked if I knew anything about the MG, I replied "yes, it is a Motor car." Well the chap replied. "As you have road that thing all the way from Norfolk, we thought you should be able to help".

The chap explained, the Dynamo had been taken off to get it repaired, they had replaced it, and now it will not start, the garage in Chorley had, to no avail, been able to get it going. If I remember correctly, the Dynamo was part of the gear mechanism to the overhead camshaft, from the crankshaft. He gave me the book to look at, the diagram showing the valve overlap etc.

Well I replied, "I can set the camshaft up to a basic setting quite easy". With the No one piston on top, I clamped the cam shaft down with the valves on the rock, turned the engine one complete turn, and set the distributor, points just open on No one piston and said, "Try it".

It fired and ran first time, "you may need to go a tooth up or down", I remarked. I was talk of the row and all I done was basic engine timing.

The reader may find this boring, but this is my story.

Next Morning all loaded up and away, the gentlemen from the hairdressing shop saw us off in amazement. Treasa on the pillion, Linda and Carrol in the side car, spare tyre's wedged over the front of the side car, we had a good ride home, in about Nine hours.

Teresa found another lady looking for out of season shelter, and again was a soft touch. The lady worked for Butlings, in Wales, during the Holiday season. How she ever come to Hindringham, I shall never know, unless Mother in Law, had something to do with it. I do remember saying she could take up the potatoes in the garden for me, she wanted me to pay her to dig them up.

Langham closed in 1958. Mr Barkley had sold me his Austin Seven Ruby, for thirty pounds and arranged for me to go to work in a Fakenham Garage.

Teresa had now work in the Chocolate Box restaurant in Fakenham I was doing a Correspondence course, to improve my technical knowledge. While attempting modifications to the Caster Camber angles, on the standard Vanguard at Langham, and having difficulties in understanding the Decimal system, I decided to improve my knowledge in that field.

It cost quite allot of money, I could pay weekly. The course included Mathematics Phase one and two. Applied Mechanics. And general Theory.

Now with our new found lodger Alice, that was her name, I could get on with my study, Teresa had another part time job in a Public house in Binham, the next Village. Life goes on, though the weekly income less, than that needed to make ends meet.

Now we had council house rent to pay, income required, was minus about a pound. I took to sweeping Chimney's, and doing the occasional motor cycle repair, we managed even a second hand black and white Television .

I went to work in the garage of R.C.E . Edmondsons LTD of Fakenham . My new job was in the Car repair side, the other chap taken on for this Contract with the American Air Force, was Desmond Hewitt.

He and I were to see to the servicing of the Standard Vanguard Vehicles on the base, and any Modifications to their fleet of Vehicles .

I was living at the time at No 10 the Elms Hindringham and using the Austin Ruby I bought from Mr Barclay at Langham. I made many modifications to it over the time I had it, by Increasing the Brake leverage, I was then making my own stick on brake linings, way before it became a Commercial proposition. I had now a home-made Lathe, made from the old sewing machine, heavily weighted, with a lead flywheel.

This helped when remetaling the big end bearings, some not badly worn could be repaired by a soldering technique and finally scraped in.

The other spare engine I had, was fitted with shell bearings. During one of my excursions into the engine I left out the splash guards from the space between the block and the crankcase. The only time I had for these jobs were on Sunday, Saturday was doing odd jobs like Chimney sweeping .

The wage I was bringing home always fell short of the outgoing bills, one needed an extra few shillings to manage. If I had no second hand part, for whatever I was doing, it had to be made. But not all my motoring was essential tinkering.

I had windscreen washers, long before they were found on production model cars, I made mine from an old fire extinguisher. I had a heater made from a large funnel fitted to the rear of the radiator, I had to cut some off the fan to make it fit, the only fault with that, was behind another vehicle, you got his exhaust into the car as well.

I had two tone air horns, made from two cycle bulb horns, a tank connected to the suction side of the manifold gave enough vacuum to suck the reads of the horn, the result being the same as blowing, the reed in the horn knew no different, this did not last long the pressure on the tank soon crushed it.

I was not deterred, by fitting two separates six-volt horns and two buttons I was able to announce my coming with two tones.

I had also a motor cycle, an Ariel red hunter, I used at times. Another old friend from Langham was at the garage, Jock Smith from Cley. He worked in the HVG side with Des Hewit, Jock was in the garage with me at Langham during the none Flying winter Months.

I made quite a reputation as a mechanic, I had studied the Theory for some years, and had some advantage that way, also found the job more a hobby than work, and I had a natural ability with mechanical things.

I was sent to Fords on a course on the new B35 Automatic gear box that was now to be used on light cars . I was one of the first MOT inspectors, when that started it cost 12 Shillings for the certificate and labour charge. Its over £30 now.

A local Gentleman one of our customers, had taken delivery of a Facel Vega. A french car very expensive £5000 you could get a Jaguar for £3000 then. It had the Crysler Typhoon V8 engine, and the ill-fated BRM gear box. I did have to change a few of them, they use to shed a tooth off the lay shaft. I went to Whaltham on Thames, to the garage of WH motors, George Abagassie one of the old Brooklands men.

I lived at the Wheat Sheaf Hotel, during my stay with WHM. Many of the Stars from the nearby film studios used the Hotel, it was a very nice place close to the water.

Strangely I did not feel myself, out of depth, though I could only afford one small glass of ale during the evenings. I spent most of the fine evenings walking by the River.

The garage was Agent for Aston Marton, I was able to learn quite a 'lot about the Facel Vega there.

On my return, I was to look after the Facel of our customer. later I was appointed, In charge of Vehicle repair. On the Sales side.

By now I had quite a name in the vehicle servicing repair tuning field. I had completed many complete rebuilds.

From time to time a new car being delivered to the garage from Fords, was in an accident, resulting in a whole new body shell needed. Those jobs I quite enjoyed, I usually insisted I complete the whole job, with the exception of the paint shop work.

I had great hopes with the completion of my Correspondence Course, to apply for one of the places of Garage Manager, that was now being advertised by one of the large oil Companies.

However, this is not to be, my life as I had planned collapsed overnight. Teresa unbeknown to me had become attached to another, took the children back home and left. I was now alone .

Church cottage Thurning will be my next tale

Thurning 1960

A settled down Family life with prospects had now become a dream of the past.
Having found Church Cottages at Thurning and purchased them hopefully I can create a new life.

Church Cottage had been Condemned, and much work needed to be done. Not only the

garden, that consisted of the two gardens and the plantation, or what remained of it. All the Oaks had
been cut down and very little plantation with the exception of a large beach tree, and the Apple trees, the total was point nine of an acre. Each week I received my pay, some nine pounds a week From the Garage I worked in Fakenham. C.Edmondsons. I bought more cement and materials needed to do the repairs to the house. There were no Council grants in those days, I also planted all the Fir and other trees that now stand around Church Cottage. The Fir trees I bought and carried home on my cycle in a large bag, they were planted out in the garden first and cared for until large enough to be planted on, and then into the final position's. Father came down and helped with some of them, so he has like I. Something to hold in our Memory. The land had to be cleared of shrub first it was quite a big job. Elder had grown up the walls of the cottage. It all had to be dug out. The footing's cleared and drainage put in, I hope the Elder Fairy understood it had to be done, and it would not impair my luck in the future. Well one dose thinks about those things having been brought up surrounded with superstitions.

But I must not dwell upon this. I am trying to record what I found to my interest in Thurning. some of the thoughts turned up and the capers I got up to from time to time.

[me at Thurning church]

My first impression as I sat with my cup of tea, in the living room at Church Cottage was. One of peace I had just been through a very tormenting period, life had collapsed I was trying to rebuild not only my life, but the house. looking back I owe much to Church Cottage.

At that time, I had none of my belongings at the house, just my cup and the kettle, water came from the well in the garden. It was getting dark. The twilight and the smell of the damp whitewash on the walls mingling with years of flour paste holding the old wallpaper to the walls, a smell I have known many times was very comforting, Outside the stillness, one could hear it. Also, though I did not realize it, the noise of my Tinnitus ringing in my head was deafening.
The results of Aero plane engine noise, and the exhaust beat of the Locomotives. I used to work with on the LNER railway.

At the time we never took notice to the damage that may happen to one's ears, neither was there any protective aids, and to wear gloves on one's hands would prove unmanly. Hence the skin on my hands today that splits in the wintertime.
Eventually I moved into Church Cottage. I made my acquaintance with the Rector the Rev Eastern, his Farther had also been the Rector there when he was a lad. He spoke of his Mother and his brother. I do not know if there were more in the family.

Thurning had been a very prospective place. There were lots of small plots. They were land of the Church called Tithes, being that they were tied to the Church. later to be called Glebe land.

I did during my stay record all written word as Church warden at the time. And before all the gravestones were removed. This was sent to the records office at Norwich. I often wondered if they escaped the big fire some years ago that destroyed many of the stored records.
The request to Church wardens for these records, came from the Diocese so perhaps some were healed by them.

The Tithes. In 1837. There were some 1584 Acre of land at a rent of 400 pounds payable to the Rector.

In my time it was referred to as the Glebe and much had gone into private hands. It is a pity the names of the lots have gone out of use. Names like Middle Lings. Pulk hole plantation, Ladies hole plantation. The Peninsula. Just to mention but a few. They are still on record should one

care to look. There was a poor law union, that took in an area of land enclosed by the road named Sandy lane down to the Blackwater river bridge and following the river up to Thurning Hall. Then up the road back to Sandy lane. I expect part of the rewards from this land were for the poor of the
parish.
There was an annual amount for blankets for the poor. In my time it was given annually in Coal at Christmas time. I was not the parish Clerk so I can only say what I believe was so at the time.
A lady from Briston left money for the church heating. A Mrs Talor she was a regular Church attendant and walked every Sunday to the services.
Her gravestone is to the left of the Church door.

The Rector and I looked into the possibilities of heating the Church with Electricity. The same that was in the Church at Sheringham. I looked into the Sherringham Installation and told the Rector of my findings. He also enquired into the possibilities. And the outcome was the Electricity company's survey. Reported that the whole installation needed replacing. But of course, the money was for the heating only and could not be used for any other purpose. And the whole thing was dropped.

The old stoke hole was still intact, but I understood the flue was bad and it was unsafe to use. Otherwise it would have been my pleasure to get it going again. I remember as children we would walk over the grid to feel the warmth from the stoke hole when attending Church.

In 1886 there was still a very large plantation of over three and a half Acre over the road from the Church. It was still there in 1930 it has all gone now. We would gather chestnuts in the Autumn, were we able to get into the wood on our way down to the Church from the rectory.

The old road they started just past Burnt house farm on the Craymere road and came out behind the stable in the Church yard. This I saw on a very old Map, so I know that to be true. The Map of 1886 shows an abundance of Oak trees all along the hedges of all the fields. There were a large number taken from Thurning in the year 1582 to 1584.

This brings me to the old bridge that I believe was a dam in the river down by the road bridge and the Meadows.

The meadows below the Church where we spent hours, looking at the wildflowers. Then there were Orchards in abundance Meadow sweet, wild Flag Iris by the stream. Where the children who visited us would play in the water to no ill effect, the water cress we gathered for tea, also took it to my Mother. The Curlew cried their haunting call up and down the meadow, Golden Plover amusing to watch protecting their young, by pretending to have broken a wing leading anyone away from the brood. We saw Water Rail. At night we heard the Night Jar calling. Fox would Bay on their way down to the woods lower down. Moor Hen nest on the bank of the stream, small Trout and Cray fish glide through the eddies.

The Cray fish I saw after finding piles of crab like deposits on the bank, where the Heron had been fishing. Reporting this to one local Naturalist he remarked how surprised he was to find them so far up stream. Frog Spawn in early March in abundance. All this before they decided to drain the Meadows. They excavated deep drains to either side of the meadows and some across. Not that it was any real success. As later when the land was seeded and the corn ready to harvest, the Machine was not able to move over much of the land due to the still boggy places. But I very much doubt the flowers will return.

The other side of the road, another meadow that had the same but not so severe treatment, was being Farmed to a certain extent. One day when Lenny Hardingham was cleaning out the river, he came across some brick structure. He had seen it before and said it was the old bridge.

After getting into the stream I had my doubts about that. It may have been the means of crossing the stream, by bridging the brick work. Though to be more than a temporary arrangement did not make reason for such a substantial structure. The time saved against the what must have been very difficult walking over the field was small.

Looking at the upstream structure, it was built curving outwards from parallel walls to the stream, some six to seven foot high, the downstream end butted back in at a sharp angle to face the water coming downstream, on the face of the butted end was two identical shapes that could have been the supporting groins for a door to be closed to hold back the water. It was in all purposes to me a Dam. Though locally I could get no one to support my theory.

I contacted the Norwich Museum. Who sent a young man, A very young man from Gressinghall Rural life Museum to see me? I told him my theory about the dam. He assured me at that time they were not making those bricks. I reminded him of Moses and the brick making. I am sure he was surprised not to have found me chewing straw and falling over the hem of my smock.

I have three theories about the use of the dam. In the years 1882 to 1884 it is written. _The Pier at Sheringham received no less than. 30 Oaks from Gresham. 500 from Thurning. 920 from around and about Baconsthorpe. Baconsthorpe being the home of the appointed force for the defense of the Coastal area.

To load all those Oaks from Thurning. Needed not only a means to get them on to the transporting vehicle, also they had to be moved to that position.

The stream either side of the road and beyond looks quite straight, one may say in places man made. Or at least man shaped to have the appearance of a canal. A Dam in that position would give ample water for not only moving large quantity of timber but, getting it up high enough to get the vehicle below it. The road bridge was not there then, and the bed of the stream much lower. Also, the downstream could have been raised from the old sheep dip at Blackwater bridge. Only in much later year's sheep dipping became a law. My Great Great Grandfather Old John Jackson Farmer and Veterinary. Invented the sheep dip, though never recorded the Patent, some other person I understand made the claim. Old John I am to believe was not very pleased.

The road bridge as it is now, was rebuilt in 1914. I found traces of a brickwork roadway under the bridge. I expect this an early attempt to make passage through the river easier. I do remember the trouble that the ford at Craymere gave to passing carts, that got stuck in the ford at flood water times.

My second theory regarding the dam. Is that in view, that the stream seemed straight for long stretches. And the means of transporting corn to the Mill would lend itself, to be an early water transport to and from the Mills.

Again, this may have been used in washing sheep there was an abundance of sheep thereabouts, and the other wash pit was up near the new Mill at Craymere.

Thirdly with the oncoming of more livestock with the Enclosure and having to slaughter much of this stock by the winter. The quantity of fodder being barely enough to see them through the winter. To flood the surrounding land during the worst of the winter, would protect the grass from the worst of the frosts. Also give an early flush of grasses in the early spring.

The first survey of 1885 shows nothing of any structures on the stream. But it does show the opening up of the stream near the old Barn. This was supposed to have been caused by a bomb from a Zeppelin during the first World War unless of course it landed in the same place.

There was another sheep wash, later a dip by the Railway bridge at Blackwater. We blocked it up and swam in it as children. There was also a number of Bombs dropped during the second world War. At Bully hills. known earlier as Bulwa hills they fell by the hedge separating the field of Mr. Fisher and the piece known as Bully hills, and two on the road. The hedge was slashed through for yards at the base and hung by supporting saplings either side. The only fatality was the rabbits living in the hedge bottom. I am sure shrapnel can still be found there today.

The Icehouse still stands today in the wood just by the turning into the Rectory. Ice was cut from the lake during the winters and stored there until required. Some people think the food was stored there as well. But I expect Ice boxes were used in the Hall as were common in Europe, When I was in Greece in the late forty's in the RAF. The Ice taken out as required.

Getting back to the Church. _I was the Church warden_. The Reverent Eastern had other parishes to see to, he had only his old cycle. I had a motorcycle and side car. On Sundays, I with the Rev Eastern in the side Car, would sally forth with gown flowing in the wind to wherever he was needed for Holy Communion.

He told me tales of how he and his Brother, in a room above the old stables. Made soap and sold it around the parish. The residue from the process again sold as a kind of scoring powder. All the proceeds to a charity. On the wall of this room you could still see where the smoke had blackened the walls. Written on the wall in large letters. The Soap Makers   He told of how they. His Brother being the Engineer as he put it. Decided to lighten up the Rectory. First the kitchen. The candles were not giving enough light. I think they allowed themselves the luxury of a one burner oil lamp in the living room.

An old Carbide lamp container was used to form the drip of petrol onto a Gauze in the lower half of the old lamp. This being the basis of the whole thing. All it needed was some gentle pressure to drive those fumes along a pipe to a jet in the kitchen. Outside a large bath full of water. A smaller bath upside down; floating and weighted, gave that pressure. The whole connected and presto a lighted jet in the kitchen. A little smelly; until a gauze mantel was obtained giving quite a good light. The last time I was at the Rectory, the pulley for raising the top bath was still there. I rely think the Ingenuity of the whole thing, really needs to be mentioned.

On my arrival at Thurning. The Church Clock had been silent for many years, the weights for the strike and the clock movement were down through the bottom of their respective boxes and laying on the vestry floor. The cables to the pulley's were broken. The case itself though, a glass cabinet had allowed quite a lot of Pigeon droppings to get into the movement. The floor of the clock room was a foot deep in droppings. I blocked up the places where the birds were getting in. The floor Isabella and I cleared much later; there were some twenty or so large bags of it. A good well dried manure for our garden. With much effort I was able to get the weights up into the clock room with the exception of the larger one. There being a number of weights to each pulley. Luckily the wires had broken at the fastening end. I was able to splice the ends; the movement was all still workable, but the escapement was short of about three pawls. The breaking of the Pawl's seemed to be the cause of the Clock running away with itself and the weights smashing down to the vestry below.

I took the escapement out. And from the pawl's left intact was able to make a pattern. Shape and braze three more into place. After reassembling and a little oil, I loaded up the weights and the old clock was running again. And kept reasonable time except for the times in the winter when I was unable to get over to wind it up in the dark. I asked the Reverent If he could do just that, but he always forgot,

It worked well without the other large weight, so It remained on the Vestry floor. The clock ran well for many years until the screws holding the hand into the driving squares came lose and fouled the other hand. It needed a very long ladder, or some means of getting up to the hands to drive back the screws or replace them. From the parish I was unable to enlist any help or a ladder, so the old clock stopped. And was still silent the day we left Thurning.

It is going again now I often wonder how much it cost to have the screws put back. It has been painted and looks nice. I did remove the escarpment drive gears to the hands to prevent an occurrence of the initial fault. These I left in the clock case, so this may have caused a little brain work. I have not been to Collage or have any Degrees. In fact, I hardly went to school. I find I can do most things with no problem, in fact if I want a job done well. I find to do it myself is the only sure way of it being done with any degree of satisfaction.

 The Reverent Eastern and I did not get on very well after I remarried, something he did not believe in. He would not give Blessing to our Marriage. From then on, we drifted apart, those were his views I did not blame him for that. Mind you I suppose he had never met anyone before who did not always agree with his views. We often had heated discussions and parted agreeing to disagree on many occasions.

[me]

I spent many hours in the Church. It was always my refuge and during the very hot summer in the cool of the pews I could snooze away the heat of the day. Also, under the river bridge with my feet in the water was quite a pleasant pastime. I am afraid if one done that today there would be a possibility of one's feet dropping off due to the pollution. There was one case just before we
left Thurning, where we found many dead fish, lots of young trout, those we gathered up in case the Heron ate them.

I lost seven Hives of Bees through the water getting Chemicals into it; from a spray machine filling its tanks from the stream; then allowing it to overflow into the side drains, Where the water being still, the Bees were getting water and taking it back to the hives. I made my complaints to all the relevant departments with the evidence. Only to be forwarded to each department in turn and back to the department I first started with. The Beekeepers Association. We stopped eating the water cress after that.

Thurning has its Ghost's. There was one in the second cottage up at Craymere beck. The cottage I lived in on two separate occasions. The neighbors would question my Mother about it she told us in later years. Often It would come into the conversation especially at Christmas, as she was relating tales of bygone years. Yes, she told the neighbor the old man follows me up to bed at night and down the stairs in the Morning. She had of course seen nothing she told us and would have been delighted had she have seen something. My Mother and her father were rely interested in such phenomenon. And many of her tales I have recorded elsewhere.

But of course, there was a ghost. A lady not old; though she looked about the age of my mother's younger sisters, but not the same features obviously. I slept in the small back room with my brother. In this room was Fathers small bookcase on a small table. We all had fears of the dark in those days, and with dimly lit rooms made it more so. A small oil lamp burning on the table in front of the bookcase was comforting, many times I woke during the night, and before the bookcase was this Lady. Just standing their hands toward the lamp as though to warm them. On these occasions I slowly pulled the bed covers over my head, even in those days I was always tired so was soon asleep again.

Though I will say there was always something strange about that room. I had many frightening dreams. But what I saw was quite obvious; and that I had not been dreaming about.

Years later when I was living in the same house, and Linda was with us then, I have talked about

Linda she came at three years old. She also slept in that room. After we left Craymere and were living at Hindringham. Linda now some ten years old asked the question. Who! was that lady who lived with us at Craymere Beck? And related the scene as I saw it all those years ago.

It seems very strange to me for it not to be the same apparition. It seems to me the Lady only Visits Children in that room.

Another spectacular one was. During my very early days at Church Cottage; I had the van. Well it had been a van and I bought it for seven pounds, the price it was bought in at. From the garage that I worked. The body was very bad, it had been a Bakers van and suffered from regular washing out; inside. I built a partition behind the driver's seat. Making quite a large cab with window to the rear. I cut the remaining part of the van off, made a wooden book for the back like a small pick-up truck, half of a lorry tire served as mudguards bolted to the underside of the book. The lads at work called it Bobtail. It was a very good little truck and I travelled many miles with it. The large cab was ideal for my Tuba that I was playing in the, _Fakenham Town band_. The night in question I had been to band practice after work and on the journey home it was raining very heavy all the way. After passing Hindolveston gate house. I saw a figure just by the old tin barn. I seemed to recognize the figure, I pulled up and he got in. The noise from the rain and the difficulty in seeing where I was going. Little if anything was said.

At the Rectory corner; I stopped with instinct and opened the door. I could not recall anyone getting out and no one was standing by the truck as one might expect. Perhaps a cherry wave and thanks.! But no. Puzzled, I made the remaining short distance home. Still puzzled; I was sure he was to be dropped at the Rectory. However, I put it down to being very tired and tried to forget all about it.

It was some months after that; the night was black. I had been to band practice again. Just before the gatehouse the heavens opened up, the rain bounced off the road the noise on the tin roof was deafening, by the tin barn was a figure I seemed to recognize, the water was teeming down his face.

a face I thought I should know, but could not bring a name to it, he was wearing glasses, that with the rain reflected in the headlights. The figure was brighter than the road before me. It did not register at the time though. I leaned over and opened the door. With the kind of doors, I had, this one had to be opened from the inside. My intended passenger climbed in dripping wet. The noise from the rain as usual made any kind of communication to say the least difficult. At the rectory I stopped leaned across the figure and opened the door. The rain was soaking my hand and forearm, no one was there. The figure that had been sitting on the seat beside me, _Soaking wet_. Not only had disappeared but; had left not a spot of water anywhere. The seat was dry the floor was dry. The only thing wet was my arm; in opening the door. To this day I will never know why I stopped at the Rectory. In retrospect I believe I knew my passenger in his mortal life, but this is between he and I.

I had two friends in the band and would come out on occasions to Thurning. The three of us would play for the Hymns in the Church, Sue on tenner horn and Peter on Cornett myself on Flugel horn. At other times on my own played the Flugel for Hymns, there being no Organist. This was up to the time I was remarried.

Thurning church

I replace a few of the leaded windows, that was just deterioration. I do not think we had any vandalism, only at the later years, some photographs I had in the Church for sale and some Hymn books were taken and thrown over in the fields on the Briston road. I made good some of the steps up to the pews, that had become rotten, excavated the hole in the wall for the wall safe. That was also attacked but not broken into on the previous occasion. All in all, I have left my mark on Thurning Church. Oh! yes one large Chestnut tree came down on the North side of the Church. I replaced the slates and repaired the rainwater gutter. I took the wood for my fire in exchange. I thought it was my due.

The old Church is full of history, if it would only talk. The pews just inside the door. The Rector said they were for the hall servants, that they may come to Church behind there betters, and leave before them to be back at the hall to greet them home.

I think that a little far-fetched, more likely to reduce the time the servants were in the company of their betters having not been called upon to do so.

On the right a row of hat pegs and benches for the men. The ladies sat on the left bench seats. The Rector also assured me the personal pews were to keep the betters from the draughts. Not to separate them from the serfs who if they were not in their seats before there betters arrived, or not in Church at all, without a very good reason; were in for possible dismissal from there place of work. One landowner in Thurning saw my father riding on the harrow he was using, he wanted to rest his legs but afraid to stop the horses, was made to do it all again on the Saturday afternoon; that was his afternoon off. These were some of the things the Reverent and I did not see eye to eye about.

He was very observant in many ways, when the Colts foot came into flower on the bank by the rectory or the Creeping Forget me not, he made a point of telling me, If he had no greens, Nettles would replace them. He ate all the mushrooms he found and those I gave him and showed me how to tell the ones that were not good to eat. Those large puff balls he said were very good, he told me how to prepare them. I did and was very surprised how nice they were.

Bees in the Church Tower. A colony of Bees attracted my attention one day flying quite densely near to the top of the Tower. It was then I realized there was a colony of Bees resident in there. I told my friend Jack Wiggans, a beekeeper himself. He said _There had been bees in there as long as he could remember_, and people before him. But up there one would not notice them, unless they were more than usually active.

I always looked in the Spring to see how they came through the winter. Later I was Interested enough to think of possibly taking up Beekeeping and used them for many of my observations. The beginning of my Bee keeping notes regarding pollen collection and the flowers from whence it came, also a makeshift hive attempting to attract some to take up residence.

One day after I had taken up Beekeeping and had been involved in taking a few Swarms of my own, I saw a swarm issuing from the Tower. After some time, it settled on the face of the Tower, I watched it for some time, It did not leave the wall and after some time returned to the tower. There was something up, perhaps the Queen failed. Next day another came out and the size of it it was obvious that the swarm of the previous day were with them.

Swarming is a predetermined. Where and when is decided well before it happens.

The air was full of Bees and to make matters worse one of my hives was swarming also, they massed and formed at a large Hazel bush behind the Church, when settled it was a good four foot around it, realizing some had been out the day previously I decided to have nothing to do with them.

Dry Bees are Bees that have swarmed and overnight used up some of the stored food they came out with in the swarm. Therefore, are now again able to bend and sting. That is why one has little trouble with a new swarm, there belly's full and happy with the new adventure. I had hoped by morning they would have gone. But it took two days before they decided to leave.

Another time the swarm was forming on the wall I decided to take them. The only way was from the top of the Tower the swarm being about six foot below the edge. A skep and ropes were fashioned into a sling, lowered down below the swarm and gradually pulled up to the swarm; now flowing into the skep. Maybe I should have lowered the skep down onto them and left it for them to crawl up into the skep and lowered it later. But it was too late now, a snag on the wall caused the skep to falter. The bees in the skep came straight up the wall, luckily, I had left the hatch open in the tower and made it with only a wing to spare. The cracks in the cover that seconds before were lit by daylight, now were black no light could be seen. Hastily I made my exit not only from the tower but the Church. I decided a few days must pass before I collect the gear I had left behind.

We spent many happy hours watching Nature and her ways. I was writing to Keith Skipper regarding a Hedge Hog we found, very small and obviously so undernourished it would not stand Hibernation. Nature of course knows this, and a marauding Blue Bottle had laid its Eggs in the ears of the poor creature, nature had provided a living host for the lava of the Fly. The Eggs would hatch and the Lava feed on the living host.

Nature is a cruel master, but this time it had a chance. We removed the fly Eggs off the Hedge Hog, made a little box in the green house, made sure there was ample food and water he was obviously getting fatter. The progress I related to Keith Skippers program from time to time, but before he was into his Hibernation some of the spines began to fall off his little body, and not long before he was balled. The Hedge Hog tale had now become so interesting to the Radio listeners. That Keith was asked how Spine less Norman was getting on, when he was out in the street. Spineless Norman as he was now called never Hibernated. He made it through to the Spring coming out of his little box to feed all winter. Even the Ministry of Agriculture sent someone to Photograph him and take a small flake of skin for analysts. When at last he Died we placed him in the garden, we could not bear to have him go for, Postmortem as the Ministry requested.

Another of my pastimes was the weather. I corresponded with Michel Hunt of Anglia Television Weather. Any unusual phenomena I may see or hear to that matter. I would record and pass on to him. He always replied even though it may have been something of little interest.
It was a sad loss when Michel died some years ago.
I would watch for the small wind twisters. Miniature tornadoes that frequent the countryside, though not so apparent as during the summer when the corn has been harvested, and the straw having been drawn up leaving the tell tail evidence.   One started in a field by the Rectory, took up straw and bouncing its way over two fields gathering more straw as it passed, entangling the wires passing over the field, the changing temperature over the Church and surrounding trees causing the force to recede and letting the straw fall all over the Church and my garden, only to pick up momentum as it passed out over another harvested corn field.

Once one spots them, more are easier to find, of course the days when those towering clouds are plummeted upwards, especially towards the direction of the sea one can expect to see them. I saw one on my way home one day, it it had crossed before me on the road at Bullyhills, and was out on the Norwich road, and no less than thirty foot across it. I could tell the size by comparison to the Bus then also on the same spot. The height many times greater and twisting off to infinity.
In the Guinness book of weather facts and feats, you will find my report of the 1St to 2Nd of December 1975. A swarm of Tornadoes over East Anglia. I picked up its path at Hindolveston, where it picked up a whole Garage carried it for many yards depositing it on the old Railway Station buildings. Passed on to Craymere Beck where it twisted the old Blacksmith shop, that at the time was full of bailed straw, the walls were twisted, and the falling roof supported on the straw inside.
It moved on to the Willows on the Reepham road where it left evidence of its passing by twisting of branches of trees by the crossroads. Many other small items I passed on, but always received with the same enthusiasm as the important ones.

Craymere Beck Blacksmith shop. The old building had many happy memories for me, we played there as children, it was there Billy Hannent was badly injured. A potato marker was standing up in the barn, a large piece of equipment for marking out the rows of potatoes, the pointers were metal tipped, and one of those entered his cheek as it fell. He was rushed into our house and the local Doctor called. Mother gave him some cake to eat after she had cleaned up the wound. You could see the cake through the wound in the flesh. I always remember that. This happened about eleven in the morning, it was four in the afternoon by the time the doctor arrived to stitch him up, it took fourteen stitches. The Doctor charged Mother sixpence, in those days you had to pay for Medical attention.

At the moment I must draw a close to my Thurning memory's, though doubtless I will return.

CITIZEN BAND RADIO
Short range Communication facility, (around 27MHZ) used by the public of the USA and many European Countries to talk to one another or call for Emergency assistance.

Use of a form of Citizen Band called open channel, above 928 MHZ, was legalized in the UK in 1980.

Prior to legalisation there were approximately half a Million Illegal operators in the UK alone using, AM on Forty Channels, 26.965 MHZ to 27.405 MHZ, called the (Naughty Forty!) these Channels were currently in use in the USA and many other countries.

Despite heavy fines, adverse press publicity and harassment by Busby, (the Police and Customs) nothing could stop it becoming a reality in this Country.

The Home Office tried to stop CB (Citizen Band) being used, warnings of prosecution and confiscation of the property housing and equipment of the operator, All sorts of excuses used to try and close these illegal CB stations, The Pirate Radio Ships were used by the Authorities against CB trying to close them down, declaring that CB would cause interference to TV and Radio broadcasts, the lack of Air space and the cost of policing was all used to try to get these Citizen Band Illegal station off the Air.

Meanwhile in the USA where CB was already a fact, the US Government introduced it as a matter of course, they argued that CB was harmless and it might prove popular, so why not let people use it.

At that time 27MHZ AM was being used, the problem with 27MHZ AM, was that at certain times of the day and particularly during the eleven-year Sun spot cycle maximums, transmissions intended for only a few miles, had the habit of turning up thousands of miles away.
However, despite its technical drawbacks 27MHZ became international accepted as the Citizen Band.

In the USA CB came into its own, when the Energy crisis struck the States.

The American Government introduced a Mandatory 55MPH speed limit, CB became a useful tool not only for locating Garages for fuel that was in short supply but dodging those 55MPH speed traps.

But here in the UK the British Government promptly band the use of CB, this curious piece of legislation made it, Illegal to use CB radio sets, but perfectly legal to own or sell them.

Around the mid seventy's, the odd CB set began to be smuggled in from the USA, gradually the build-up of CB breakers around the Country took place, the Police had better things to do than chase Illegal CB breakers around the Country " first they had to catch them in the act using the Transmitter to transmit with", so they left them alone.

Although CB was growing fast, the band of illegal users was still small, most people did not know CB existed.

Programs on British Television Emanating from the USA built up the British public's awareness of CB, still only a small band of breakers enjoyed their Illegal CB, however a record by, C W Mackall, called Convoy was being played in Britain especially from the Pirate Radio stations who encouraged by the Government to ban CB, the language was weird and not much of a song, but it certainly done a great job for CB, suddenly the Media started talking about, Cab=over=Pete' and explained that the 'reefer' he had on, had nothing to do with drugs, but was CB lingo.

The Media became interested in CB, a whole new sub culture caught the imagination of the British youth, overnight everyone wanted CB, except of course the Government, who quickly dusted down the familiar excuses that were used against commercial Radio, but it was too late.

By the early Eighty's there were already a million breakers on the air and once again the Government had been caught. Despite screams of anguish from the Post Office and even bigger screams from the Home Office, the Government instructed the Civil Service to "look into the matter" and announced they would circulate draft regulation shortly.
Naturally everyone started buying rigs like mad, the CB shops started springing up all over the place, although supposedly selling accessories only, many were offering a vast array of American rigs under the counter, The Home Office draft,
issued in a green paper which came out late Nineteen Eighty entitled "Open Channel a discussion document" came as a big shock to everyone, they subjected a frequency that was so high most manufactures didn't know it existed.

The cost of producing rigs on the suggested frequency 934 MHZ would be around ú200-ú300, and the range would be little more than shouting distance, rallies were organised, demonstrations ensued, and questions were asked in the House.

Finally, after wavering around 22 Channels on Half a Watt, they announced the system as it finally was and still is today, to save face they suggested the 27MHZ system should run in tandem with the higher, far more costly 934 MHZ system.
At that time myself unable to afford a rig, but always interested in Radio, and an interested Short wave listener was able to, listen in on some of the local CB stations especially in the evenings, apart from some misgivings found the operators on the nets that were now springing up, interesting and something we would like to be part of.

Purchasing our first Rig from the garage at Thursford, the fun then began, the first Antenna was a Wot Pole, that was mounted on top of a long pole cut from the nearby wood, the radiating element had to be moved up and down until the correct match was found to the Radio, quite a few trips up and down that pole before a match was found, many stations were doing the same thing, and much of the conversation over the Air was along that subject, finally most were set up satisfactory, and in the evenings Nets began to spring up on certain frequency's.
 As things settled down, the Nets containing the same people and the Forty channels most evenings were occupied, one person taking part as the leader and passing transmitting to the next, conversation could be anything from the aches and pains to what had been going on in their day, sometimes a quiz would take up the whole evening, any one flicking through the Channels and thinking they would like to take part, would at a brief interval call "Breaker on the side" and mostly would be called in, to give his or her name and location,
The villages and Towns took on their own Names, Briston was called Piston town, because of the small vehicle engineering works at the West End, Holt was The Owls, Fakenham took on Omaha and had quite a strong club with a regular weekly meeting, it was not long before most breakers had a rig in the Car and serving the community in many ways.

We were a little apprehensive at first, one afternoon Isabela switched on the Rig to listen and found three ladies talking, the subject she found interesting, at a pause during the conversation Isabela pressed the Microphone key and said Hello, and was requested "Come in breaker"
What is your handle "CB Name" I am Emerald Isle and we have Moona one and Silver Bird, in turn they introduced each other, and decided to christen Isabela" Poo Bear" as at the time I was keeping Bees, and that was our first introduction into taking an active part in the CB community, many a friend ship sprung up from those days and one in particular was Emerald

Isle living then in Wroxham, and to this day are still friends and still communicating at least once a week be it though now by Telephone.

The Evening nets became a regular thing for us our net on 39 was with breakers at Melton Briston Weybourne Kelling Holt and others that may join in, our various hobbies were discussed for myself I was studying for my City and Guilds and one or two others following the same path into a licence for Armature Radio, and CB was a great help in doing so.

CB united people all over the country, the Sun Spot conditions that appear about every eleven years and in the eighties were at their maximum, these conditions gave the possibility to contact stations as far away as Boston and Mable Thorpe on a regular basis, a regular contact was with a Mobile station on the sea front at Mable Thorpe on a Sunday morning, at its best we were copying France and Belgium, the Light Ships out on the North Sea were some of our regular contacts, one in particular was "Safety Valve" at times during foggy weather he would say "hang on the fog horn is about to blow" some of the coasting cargo vessels had crew men who had CB with them, and would call in on the way up to Hull or back down to London.

The CB Lingo was strange at first though not all used it, clubs began to spring up and one in particular was the Fakenham Omaha club, general secretary Big D a Briston lad who raised a great deal of money for the Fakenham Medical practice in the form of Mobile Equipment accident and emergency though a very sick man himself always took the sponsored dip in the sea at Wells on Boxing day,
Big D lived at Colkirk and drove a reliant Robbin that he called a Plastic Pig.
The Breakers and their Handles were very colour full, just some of those handles and locations as I remember.

"Dipstic" Hindoleveston, "Tiger Moth" Yaxham, "Condor" Briston, "Ludwig" Briston, "Bull Ring" Southreps, "Soverien Lady" Saxthorpe, "Thunder Flash" South Reps, "Pied Piper and Hedgehog" Saxthorpe, Rough Nut Lowestoft, Esso Blue Colkirk, Romeo Foxtrot Bradenham, Blue Bird Melton, Freckle Face Corpusty, Space Shuttle Corpusty, Metal Man Colkirk, Wensum Summerton, King Arther Kelling, Wensum Flyer Swanton Novers, Model Man ?, Cromer Crab Bawdswell, Silver Surf ?, Paper Maker ?, Spotlight Corpusty, Wing Mirror Bugh Park, Sugar Fairy Aylsham, Broken Piston Holt, Duke of Norfolk Stibard, Red Arrow Christchurch, Tic Nick Aylsham, Trade Bike Briston, King Fisher Lenwade. Fly Fisher Fakenham, Zebra Fakenham, Mower Man Smallbough, Vaxhall Norwich, Lucky Dog ?, Long John Silver Kelling, MAC Melton, Cod Catcher Yaxham, Dragon Junior Felbrig, Big D Colkirk, Cannon 35 At Spanner City Thursford, Digit Mile Cross, Die Hard Kelling, Red Rose Snoring, Ram Rod North Elenham, Black

Sweed and Little Mum North Walsham, Ferrit Thursford, Teddy Bear Aylsham, Appolo Sheringham, Tweedle Dee Honey Bee King Bee Coltishal, Emerald Isle and Memory Man Cotishall, Mawkin Sharrington, Whip Line at Sea 20 mile east of Cromer, Screaming Demond and Safety Valve on a Gas rig in the north Sea, Quick brew Wells, Church Town Boy Walsingham, Rocking Robin Sherringham, Sweeny Tod Foulsham, Cano Man Wells, Snow white Wells, Sea Bird GT Whitchigham, Smoky Norway, Honky Salthouse, Wolly and Cinderella Salthouse, Medicin man Holt, Blue Flash Holt, Paratroper Kelling, Church Tower walsingham, Phanthom North Crete, Twinkel Toes Aylsham, Kidney Bean Repham, Liquid Gold Norwich, Rodeo Man Bunwell, Gun Barrel Norwich, Compressor Nottingham.

Just some of the Handles from one of the logs we kept during those days, can you recognise anyone, Silver spot and Smoky Joe, Doris and Joe lived in Briston CB was not just for the young, and they were not teen age's, in fact Old Age Pensioners and fine Breakers.

This part of my story starts at the Garage of RC Edmonds LTD ; things were getting where those who were able to do a good job , were being directed by those who did not .
This was happening all over the country , Whiz Kids with their degrees in Education History or Art it did not seem to matter , if they had the Documents they got the job , and this is the kind of Management we were getting , so it was to pastures green some of us were looking , people like myself who studied the theory of the job and that included an extensive Mathematical program that went with the study , paid for by myself and studied in my own spare time , A very good grounding for any Engineering problem that may come up .

Brook Hirst Igranic a firm making parts for Electrical switch gear had just started up at Melton Constable in the old Machine shop of the long gone Midland and Great Northern railway , fittingly the old shop should once again become the Machine shop , its last job was to house the wagon Sheet repair side of the old Railway .

It came to my knowledge they were looking for a Maintenance Man I applied for the post and was given an interview , the day duly arrived and at Melton I saw a Mr Ted Archer who had driven up from Bedford to Interview me .
What did I know about Capstan lathes , and other Machinery that they would be having in the work shop , I had not seen a Capstan lathe before and said so , yet by the time came for him to leave he was quite convinced I would be quite capable of looking after things there for them .

Alan Lambert and Bob Grimmer had already started work there , they had also left the garage , they were working as Setters on the Capstan Lathes , at the start there were about fifteen people including Lady's .
Ron Bettal was in charge of production John Miller was looking after Inspection , that was seeing that the items made on the Machines were within the limits of the drawings and the most important man Mr George Woodcock , George had been in from the very beginning , he made the tea , he looked after the keys and locking up .
A valuable man to have around and the lowest paid , yet this seem to be the way of things there are none more blinded than Management .
Not that Ron Bettle could change anyway , his hands were tied in that direction , I duly started work in the machine shop , I installed myself at a work bench , and after a good look round decided on a plan of routine Maintenance , It looked as though that all things that did not come under production was to be my responsibility , It was not long before I decided that I could make a nice little hidey hole for myself in the Compressor house , a little noisy but away from the workshop .
Two large Compressors that supplied the compressed Air for the Air tools and for the Capstans , George had been seeing to them , now I made this the first job of the day to start the Compressors before doing my general rounds of the Factory , the rounds that would bring to light any repairs that needed doing .

Much of the old Railway was still standing only the lines had been taken up , much of my work was outside even on the roof , the rain found its way in at times I done my best to repair the roof as well , as an old Railway building , the roof had walk ways so that was no problem , I had no fixed abode so was able to make excursions around the old Railway property , I took many Photographs of the old buildings before they were taken down , life progressed in a very sociable way .

I made modifications to the Jigs for production made up new Jigs just because I loved the challenge Next to the machine shop was the old Boiler house that had supplied the steam for the Machine shop , another of my haunts .
I also met Allan Bloom there he was getting parts for Bressingham , Ron had told me to help him where I could , he took what he wanted even gave me open invitation to Bressingham , later the remains of the boilers were taken out for scrap just leaving an empty building .
All the time the production was expanding , more machines coming for me to assemble , another shop taken on , this time the long Carriage building shop with its small ancillary workshops at the side , these I made into Offices and Canteen .

And at the far end a paint shop , all with just a little help from the odd shop worker who was out of floor work at the time , now the production was on large cases for the Resistors , another product of the company , the whole resistor could now be assembled at Melton , Large presses were now in the new shop .

The Management that had now increased by the influx of staff from the Companies recently bought up another Resistor company , Walsh " In my opinion a much simpler one than the one we were making . Yet this was later faded out , Ron Bettle Died Suddenly , now I had no real friend left , the new Management were all social climbing , trying to outshine each other , things were getting bad , much of the work on production had to be done over and over again , the scrap metal Bins became fuller and fuller , The new regime wanted things done there way , in the past the worker had told them how the job needed to be done , and put things right , now they only follow instructions ,

By now my brother was working in the large resistor shop on assembly , I was trying to get him into the Maintenance shop with me , they had just employed another chap but very unsuitable .

I gave him the large shop to look after so got him out of my hair .

Ted Archer came up one day , I want you to build an office block in the old boiler house he said , I replied I am no builder , that does not matter he said you can do anything , I replied if you say so just send me the materials and leave me to get on with it .

I had not allowed for our new management , who were supposed to let me get on with the work , I had the area all prepared for the delivery of the Concrete I wanted four inches all over , I had pegged it for that quantity , I gave the quantity required to the man who was to see to all that side for me , also I would need two wheel barrows and four shovels the day the Concrete arrived .

He continually asked me when I wanted the Concrete , the answer was the same when you get me the tools , one morning on my arrival at work there was a load of Concrete , and still no tools or labour , the Concrete had to be moved to the far side of the building , the tanker could only get it half way that is why I wanted the tools , by the time we had borrowed tools for the job the Driver had dumped the load as fare as he could get it into the building and left .

Also, our Mr Management was not available for comment , I was able to get some labour from the workshop , we proceeded to move the Concrete to the position only to find it was not going to be enough , half enough to be exact .

I tracked down Mr Management who claimed I did not need all I had ordered, and he had reordered , so that is why the floor was and I suppose still is , two and a half inches thick in the

best of places . To cap the day , after we had smoothed over the floor later having given it chance to go off a little , it rained that night .
I had previously requested repairs to the roof , now we had large holes in our new floor , all in all not a very good start to the new office all down to Management .

By now I had built one large office , two small offices , a store room Toilets , and a large entrance hall I put up a suspended ceiling , My brother joined me to work on maintenance , in time to help with the installation of the lighting , at the same time we installed our listening device into the office via the electrical conduit , which proved later to be more funny than Hancock's half hour .
The rain had made it difficult to lay the floor tiles , we pleaded for a sanding machine but to no avail , in the end we had to scrub the floor with old grindstone wheels , to get it into some kind of condition to lay the tiles , those we heated in an old oven until supple , so as to follow the irregularities of the floor , All this down to Management again , the office goes into use , we back to our work and hobbies My Brother was making a Go 'cart at the time , we also made a few repairs for a firm of potato growers , who supplied us with ample potatoes . one Summer the work force complained of flies . Hordes of little flies , they were coming off the potatoes stored nearby .
I saw the owner who remarked , I know but the belong to the potato marketing board , they are keeping them back to hold the price up , give me a written complaint and I can do something about it " Simple" you had not taken our Management into consideration .
We cannot give anything in writing say's Management giving lots of unsound reasons to why not , more complaints to us from the shop floor , then the Union .
I returned to the Management What about the Rats I remarked , to that management said the rats if any will stay with the potatoes , well what was one to do , later when they had gone home , we went up into the space above the offices and with rounded up small pieces of black pitch off the roof rounded to look like Rat droppings I dropped them down onto the desks through the small space between the light switches .
I was ready next morning as the cleaner came to the office , and expressed my surprise at what she found , also the chance of disease from handling the droppings .
I took charge of them for her , as I had expected when the Management arrived to work they were well informed , and called a meeting in the office of all concerning bodies , we on the other hand were up in the attic following the procedure , it was pathetic , one say well they are not our rats if we call the Council we will have to pay , thinking of the petty cash and lunches out I suppose , another it may be just a passing Rat , this is how it proceeded until it was decided to leave it down to a solitary Rat . After they had gone home that evening , we gave

them another good dose , I helped the lady to clean up in the morning showing Management what I had collected on my way out of the office .

Another meeting was called , that was the same as the first , but in the end decided to call the Council Being well informed we made trails in the dust to indicate Rat activity even made a nice hole in the boards and paw marks in the dust , the Rat man called Yes ! they had Rats for sure he laid down Bate and would call back , and sure enough when he came back it was all gone , he put down some more and they cleaned that up , in the end we got bored with that game , they never did find out how the work force was always well informed of their activities , there are many more tales but at the moment I will leave that part of my story

By now my brother was working in the large resistor shop on assembly , I was trying to get him into the Maintenance shop with me , they had just employed another chap but very unsuitable.

I gave him the large shop to look after so got him out of my hair .

Ted Archer came up one day , I want you to build an office block in the old boiler house he said , I replied I am no builder , that does not matter he said you can do anything , I replied if you say so just send me the materials and leave me to get on with it .

I had not allowed for our new management , who were supposed to let me get on with the work , I had the area all prepared for the delivery of the Concrete I wanted four inches all over , I had pegged it for that quantity , I gave the quantity required to the man who was to see to all that side for me , also I would need two wheel barrows and four shovels the day the Concrete arrived .

He continually asked me when I wanted the Concrete , the answer was the same when you get me the tools , one morning on my arrival at work there was a load of Concrete , and still no tools or labour , the Concrete had to be moved to the far side of the building , the tanker could only get it half way that is why I wanted the tools , by the time we had borrowed tools for the job the Driver had dumped the load as fare as he could get it into the building and left .

Also, our Mr Management was not available for comment , I was able to get some labour from the workshop , we proceeded to move the Concrete to the position only to find it was not going to be enough , half enough to be exact .

I tracked down Mr Management who claimed I did not need all I had ordered, and he had reordered , so that is why the floor was and I suppose still is , two and a half inches thick in the best of places . To cap the day , after we had smoothed over the floor later having given it chance to go off a little , it rained that night .

I had previously requested repairs to the roof , now we had large holes in our new floor , all in all not a very good start to the new office all down to Management .

By now I had built one large office , two small offices , a store room Toilets , and a large entrance hall I put up a suspended ceiling , My brother joined me to work on maintenance , in time to help with the installation of the lighting , at the same time we installed our listening device into the office via the electrical conduit , which proved later to be more funny than Hancock's half hour .

The rain had made it difficult to lay the floor tiles , we pleaded for a sanding machine but to no avail , in the end we had to scrub the floor with old grindstone wheels , to get it into some kind of condition to lay the tiles , those we heated in an old oven until supple , so as to follow the irregularities of the floor , All this down to Management again , the office goes into use , we back to our work and hobbies My Brother was making a Go 'cart at the time , we also made a few repairs for a firm of potato growers , who supplied us with ample potatoes . one Summer the work force complained of flies . Hordes of little flies , they were coming off the potatoes stored nearby .

I saw the owner who remarked , I know but the belong to the potato marketing board , they are keeping them back to hold the price up , give me a written complaint and I can do something about it " Simple" you had not taken our Management into consideration .

We cannot give anything in writing say's Management giving lots of unsound reasons to why not , more complaints to us from the shop floor , then the Union .

I returned to the Management What about the Rats I remarked , to that management said the rats if any will stay with the potatoes , well what was one to do , later when they had gone home , we went up into the space above the offices and with rounded up small pieces of black pitch off the roof rounded to look like Rat droppings I dropped them down onto the desks through the small space between the light switches .

I was ready next morning as the cleaner came to the office , and expressed my surprise at what she found , also the chance of disease from handling the droppings .

I took charge of them for her , as I had expected when the Management arrived to work they were well informed , and called a meeting in the office of all concerning bodies , we on the other hand were up in the attic following the procedure , it was pathetic , one say well they are not our rats if we call the Council we will have to pay , thinking of the petty cash and lunches out I suppose , another it may be just a passing Rat , this is how it proceeded until it was decided to leave it down to a solitary Rat . After they had gone home that evening , we gave them another good dose , I helped the lady to clean up in the morning showing Management what I had collected on my way out of the office .

Another meeting was called , that was the same as the first , but in the end decided to call the Council Being well informed we made trails in the dust to indicate Rat activity even made a nice hole in the boards and paw marks in the dust , the Rat man called Yes ! they had Rats for sure he laid down Bate and would call back , and sure enough when he came back it was all gone , he put down some more and they cleaned that up , in the end we got bored with that game , they never did find out how the work force was always well informed of their activities , there are many more tales but at the moment I will leave that part of my story

About 1980 The Management had the chance to remove me from their midst ,
I had been getting to close for comfort for some of them .
They had the chance of making me Redundant and took the golden opportunity , I had left the company within an hour of being told , such was there hurry to remove me , I was not even allowed to go back to pick up my pay and Documents , they sent it to my house , Mind you they all followed me later , but these things take time.
It was the few days before the Annual Holiday , I was to as usual work over the Holidays , jobs that could not be done when the Machines are working .
On being called to the office was informed that after the Holidays there would be some redundancy , as Union Convenor was entitled to this information , but not to say anything until after the Holiday .
After I left off work I wrote a letter to the management proposing moves that could be made to lessen the need for any Redundancy , also I was prepared to go to Bedford and put forward same to the Directors , I handed in the latter first thing on the Monday morning .

Shortly after I was informed that I was the first to go and to be off the premises within the hour.
I informed the Union who wanted not to get involved .
The Redundancy pay was not much I think we bought a new freezer with the money ; I was on the Unemployed for a year and later the welfare benefit , work was hard to come by at that time .
I had a pile of refused applications , the money was then 8.50 a week , I made good use of my enforced holiday and done all the things I had promised myself when I had the time , I made our own fuel for the fire from straw from a nearby straw yard , I collected the straw that had become aged and partly rotted , pressed it in a home-made press weighted down with a weight from a Railway points signal lever , I found the pressure had to be gradual , I was able to make three a day but the third was not removed from the press until morning .
These then laid out under a cover in the orchard , covered from any rain but open to the air , sometimes it took only two days before the blocks were ready to store or use , they were very light ; but three of the blocks on the closed fire at night were quite ample to keep the fire going until morning .
I gathered much wood from the surrounding fields , and by the winter a well-stocked shed was ready to keep us warm .

I had by now installed a closed all fuel burning stove , bought second hand for ú5 a water tank and radiators , we were quite modern in our own way , the old bucket toilet was the next to go , I made two bottomless frames about eighteen
inches square to make the slabs I would need to build the store and soakaway for a water toilet.
The sand I excavated from the garden the cement I had to buy that , with a mixture of three to one I started making the slabs , some days I was able to make three a day , I built a small house about three by five foot , next to one I had built much earlier to house the tank for the rainwater , that was pumped up from a large tank I had previously built in the garden , this supplied the water into the kitchen over the sink for washing only as the drinking water we still brought daily from the well .
Even after I had made the well water into a pumped supply up into the house we still brought the water for drinking from the well head , this was a game at times , if the roof tank was full it was possible to overflow the tank in the attic , but this did not happen too often , I had a switch that came on lighting a bulb when the tank was full , the off switch for the pump being in the kitchen near to the indication lamp .
For the toilet soil tank I excavated a large hole this was about nine by three feet and four feet deep , it was to have one tank to collect the first of the solids another to collect solids that escaped the first tank and the third as a soakaway with no bottom to it , I made covers from more slabs to enable me to inspect and clean out from time to time , I must say , all the time we used that toilet there was no smell from it or even when it had to be cleaned out did it smell offensive at any time .
Yet a professionally built sewer not far away two fields away to be exact , whenever it had to be pumped out caused a very offensive smell and one had to retire from the garden , the water for the toilet I piped from the rain water tank .
They were happy days at Church Cottage .
I decided to take up Bee keeping , I had been repairing some Beehives for Jack Wiggans , and from the left over parts of hives I made some for myself , also obtained books on the subject , I spent many hours observing the Bees from the Church tower , a colony had been there for many years I was told , I noted down there comings and goings , I watched the workers at the flowers getting the various kinds of pollen , I experimented with a makeshift hive expecting them to make a home there ; tempted by some sugar syrup .
Eventually one April I obtained a small Colony of Bees , five frames to be exact , I had made all the necessary parts like crown board to take the feeder , all I needed now was some experience and as the years went by, I got plenty of that .

Other books By Peter Jackson Langham dome Norfolk

Railway workers

Edited partly by Lynn Marie Jackson contact lynnmariejackson@aol.co.uk

Printed in Great Britain
by Amazon